HOW TO USE MARKETING TO DOUBLE YOUR PROFITS

in 6 Months or Less...

Bruce Caswell
Business & Marketing Strategist

COPYRIGHT & DISCLAIMER

How To Use Marketing To Double Your Profits in 6 months or less

Designed by Leader Publishing Worldwide - www.noresults-nofee.com
Published by Compass Publishing - www.compass-publishing.com
Printed by The Printing House - www.tphprinting.co.uk

For more copies, email: info@MaximumPerformanceAcademy.com
Further Information: www.MaximumPerformanceAcademy.com

Private Marketing Consultancy
You can consult with Bruce Caswell privately to help you double your profits or meet any of your professional or personal goals

Contact 0330 8280 866 or info@ MaximumPerformanceAcademy.com

To my family

INTRODUCTION TO THE PROFIT FORMULA

'It is not enough to do your best; you must know what to do, and then do your best'

W Edwards Deming (1990 – 1993) Visionary American Statistician and Consultant with an unwavering belief in continuous improvement

The purpose of this book is to teach you the business and marketing fundamentals needed so that you can double your profits in the next 6 months or less. If you concentrate on a few significant areas of your business and tackle them one at a time you will find that doubling your profits is easier than you think. Once you have doubled your profits, you will have the confidence to grow your business even further so that it will provide you with the life you have always wanted for you and your family. After all, that's why you started your own business in the first place wasn't it?

In this introduction, your will learn the profit formula, which can be expressed very simply like this:

- **Leads** x **Conversion Rate (%)** = Number of Customers
- No of Customers x **No of Sales** x **Average Value** = Revenue
- Revenue x **Margin** = Gross Profit
- Gross Profit *less* Overheads = Net Profit

You will notice that some of these terms are shown in **bold**. These are the aspects of the business that can be considered marketing, that are within your control and which contribute to your Gross Profit.

Net Profit takes account of the business overheads which are also in your control, and which also need to be considered as overheads can significantly impact profit. But we will concentrate on the upside profit possible from improving your marketing performance, as this has much greater potential. Don't be misled by the apparent simplicity of the profit formula. It is very powerful and, if you really understand it, it will transform the way you think about your business.

As you read the book, relate the principles that follow to the profit formula, and remember it does not matter what industry nor type of business you operate. What matters is that you grasp the heart of these principles and the underlying lessons of these strategies that can grow any operation in any category of business imaginable.

Remember too, that the best time to start is TODAY, not tomorrow, not next week or next year.

Good Luck!

Bruce Caswell

PS. Please visit www.MaximumPerformanceAcademy.com/more-profits for a further explanation of the profit formula.

QUICK CONTENTS

DETAILED CONTENTS

Chapter 3   **How to Create Effective Marketing Materials**

Chapter 4   **How to Use Testimonials & Profit from Social Proof**

Chapter 5   How to Create Immediate Sales

Chapter 6   How to Generate Unlimited Leads

Chapter 7   How to Profit from Joint Ventures

Chapter 8   How to Use Press Releases for Instant Profit

1

HOW TO DEFINE
YOUR TARGET MARKET

What is a Target Market?

Many businesses can't answer the question: *Who is your target market?* They have often made the fatal assumption that *everyone* will want to purchase their product or service with the right marketing strategy.

A target market is simply the group of customers or clients who are most likely to purchase a specific product or service. This group of people all tend to have something in common, often age, gender, hobbies, location or profession.

Your target market, then, are the people who will buy your offering and this includes your existing customers as well as those who have yet to buy from you.

Every one of your target market is motivated to do one of three things:

- Fulfil a need
- Solve a problem
- Satisfy a desire

To build, maintain, and grow your business, you need to know who your customers are, what they do, what they like, and why they would buy your product or service. Getting this wrong – or not taking the time to get it right – will cost you time, money, and potentially the success of your business.

The Importance of Knowing Your Target Market

Knowledge and understanding of your target market is the keystone in the arch of your business. Without it, your product or service positioning, pricing, marketing strategy, and eventually, your business could very quickly fall apart.

If you don't intimately know your target market, you run the risk of making mistakes when it comes to establishing pricing, product mix, or service packages. Your marketing strategy will lack direction, and produce mediocre results at best. Even if your marketing message and unique selling proposition (USP) are clear, and your brochure is perfectly designed, it means nothing unless it arrives in the hands (or ears) of the right people.

Determining your target market takes time and careful diligence. While it often starts with a best guess, assumptions cannot be relied on and research is required to confirm original ideas. Your target market is not always your ideal market.

Once you build an understanding of who your target market is, keep up with your market research. Having your finger on the pulse of their motivations and drivers – which naturally change – will help you to anticipate needs or wants and evolve your business.

Types of Markets

Consumer

The Consumer Market includes those general consumers who buy products and services for personal use, or for use by family and friends. This is the market category we fall into when we're shopping for groceries or clothes, seeing a movie, going to the theatre, or out for lunch. Retailers focus on this market category when marketing their goods or services.

Public Sector

The Public Sector Market serves society and provides products or services for the benefit of society. This includes hospitals, non-profit organisations, government organisations, schools and universities. Members of the Public Sector Market purchase products to use in the provision of services to people in their care.

Business to Business (B2B)

The B2B Market is just what it seems to be: businesses that purchase products and services from other business to run their operations. These purchases can include products that are used to manufacture other products (raw materials or technical), products that are needed for daily operations (such as office supplies), or services (such as accounting, shredding and legal).

Resellers

This market can also be called the Intermediary Market because it consists of intermediary businesses that act as channels for goods and services between other markets. Goods are purchased and sold for a profit – without any alterations. Members of this market include wholesalers, retailers, resellers, and distributors.

Determining Your Target Market

Product / Service Investigation

The process for determining your target market starts by examining exactly what your offering is, and what the average customer's motivation for purchasing it is. Start by answering the following questions:

Does your offering meet a basic need?	
Does your offering serve a particular want?	
Does your offering fulfil a desire?	

What is the lifecycle of your product / service?	
What is the availability of your offering?	
What is the value of the average customer's purchase?	
How many times or how often will customers purchase your offering?	
Do you foresee any upcoming changes in your industry or location that may affect the sales of your offering? (positive or negative)	

Market Research

On the ground

Spend some time on the ground researching who your target market might be. If you're thinking about opening a coffee shop, check the location at different times of the day to get a sense of the people who live, work, and play in the neighbourhood. Notice their age, gender, clothing, and any other indications of income and activities.

Of the competition

Who is your direct competition targeting? Is there a small niche that is being missed? Observing the clients of your competition can help to build an understanding of your target market, regardless of whether it is the same or opposite.

For example, if you own a children's clothing boutique and the majority of middle-class mothers shop at the local department store, you may wish to focus on higher-income families as your target market.

Online research

Many cities and towns – or at least regions – have demographic information available online. Research the ages, incomes, occupations, and other key pieces of information about the people who live in the area you operate your business. From this data, you will gain an understanding of the size of your total potential market.

With existing customers

Talk to your existing customers through focus groups or surveys. This is a great way to gather demographic and behavioural information, as well as genuine feedback about product or service quality and other information that will be useful in a business or marketing strategy.

Who is Your Market?

Based on your product / service and market investigations, you will be able to piece together a basic picture of your target market, and some of their general characteristics. Record some notes here.

Target Market Framework: Consumer

Market Type:	Consumer
Gender:	☐ Male ☐ Female
Age Range:	
Purchase Motivation:	☐ Meet a Need ☐ Serve a Want ☐ Fulfil a Desire
Activities:	
Income Range:	
Marital Status:	
Location:	☐ Local ☐ National ☐ Regional ☐ International
Other Notes:	

Target Market Framework: Public Sector

Market Type:	Public Sector
Organisation Type:	☐ Health ☐ Local Gov. ☐ Non-profit ☐ Agency ☐ School ☐ Church ☐ University ☐ …………..
Purchase Motivation:	☐ Operational Need ☐ Client Want ☐ Client Desire
Purpose of Organisation:	
Organisation's Client Base:	
Size:	
Location:	☐ Local ☐ National ☐ Regional ☐ International
Other Notes:	

Target Market Framework: B2B

Market Type:	Business to Business (B2B)
Company Size:	
Number of Employees:	
Purchase Motivation:	☐ Operations Need ☐ Strategy ☐ Functionality
Annual Revenue:	
Industry / Sector:	
Location(s):	☐ Local ☐ National ☐ Regional ☐ International
Purpose of Business:	
People, Culture & Values:	
Other Notes:	

Target Market Framework: Reseller

Market Type:	Reseller
Industry:	
Client Base:	
Purchase Motivation:	☐ Operations Need ☐ Client Wants ☐ Functionality
Annual Revenue:	
Age:	
Location:	☐ Local ☐ National ☐ Regional ☐ International
Other Notes:	

Your Target Market: Putting It Together

Based on the information you gather from your product / service and market investigations, you should have a clear vision of your realistic target market. Here are a few examples of how this information is put together and conclusions are drawn:

Target Market Example: Consumer Market

Business: Baby Clothing Boutique	**Business Purpose:** - ***Meet a need*** (provide clothing For infants and children aged 0 to 5 years) - ***Serve a want*** (clothing is brand name only, and has a higher price point than the competition)
Market Type: Consumer	
Gender: Women	
Marital Status: Married	
Market Observations: - Located on Main Street of Anytown, a street that is seeing many new boutiques open up, located near to the main shopping mall two blocks from popular mid range restaurant that is busy at lunchtimes	**Industry Predictions:** - Large number of new housing developments in the city and surrounding areas - Two new schools in construction - Expect to see an influx of new families move to town from Anycity
Competition Observations: - Baby clothing also available at two local department stores, and one second-hand shop on opposite side of town	**Online Research:** - Half of Anytown's population is female, and 25% have children under the age of 15 years - Anytown's population is expected to increase by 32% within three years - The average household income for Anytown is £50,000 annually

Target Market:
The target market can then be described as married mothers between the ages of 25 and 45, with children under five years old, who have recently moved to Anytown from Anycity, and have a household income of at least £60K annually.

Target Market Example: B2B Market

Business: Confidential Paper Shredding	**Target Business Size:** Small to medium sized (SME)
Market Type: B2B (Business to Business)	**Target Business Revenue:** £500K to £1M
Business Purpose: - *Meet an operations need* Provide confidential on-site shredding services for business documents	**Target Business Type:** - Produce or handle a variety of sensitive paper documentation - accountants, lawyers, estate agents
Market Observations: - There are two main areas of office buildings and industrial warehouses in Anycity with three New office towers that will be completed this year	**Industry Predictions:** - The professional sector is seeing revenue growth of 24% over last year, which indicates increased client billing and staff recruitment
Competition Observations: - One confidential shredding company operates locally - They provide regular (weekly or biweekly) service, but lack capacity to handle larger volumes	**Online Research:** - Anycity's biggest employment sectors are: manufacturing, tourism, food services, and professional services
Target Market: The target market can then be described as small to medium sized businesses in the professional sector with an annual revenue of £500K to £1M who require both regular and infrequent large volume paper shredding services.	

Segmenting Your Market

Your market segments are the groups within your target market – broken down by a determinant in one of the following four categories:

- Demographics
- Psychographics
- Location
- Behaviour

Segmenting your target market into several more specific groups allows you to further tailor your marketing campaign and more specifically position your product or service. You may wish to divide your advertising campaign into four sections, and target four specific markets with messages that will most resonate with the audience.

For example, the baby clothing store may choose to segment its target market by psychographics, or lifestyle. If the larger target market is *married females with children under five, between the ages of 25 and 45, who have a household income of at least £60K annually*, it can be broken down into the following lifestyle segments:

- Fitness-oriented mothers
- Career-oriented mothers
- New mothers

With these three categories, unique marketing messages can be created that speak to the hot-buttons of each segment. The more accurate and specific you can make communications with your target market, the greater impact you will have on your revenues.

Market Segmentation Variables

Demographic	Psychographic	Location	Behaviour
Age	Personality	Region	Brand Loyalty
Income	Lifestyle	Country	Product Usage
Gender	Values	City / Town	Purchase-frequency
Generation	Attitude	Area	Profitability
Nationality	Motivation		Readiness-to-buy
Ethnicity	Activities		User Status
Marital Status	Interests		
Family Size			
Occupation			
Religion			
Language			
Education			
Job Type			
Housing Type			
Homeowner			
Political views			

Understanding Your Target Market

Once you have determined who your market is, make a point of learning everything you can about them. You need to have a strong understanding of who they are, what they like, where they shop, why they buy, and how they spend their time. Remind yourself that you may *think* you know your market, but until you have verified the information, you'll be driving your marketing strategy blind.

Also be aware that markets change, just like people. Just because you knew your market when you started your business 10 years ago, doesn't mean you know it now. Regular market research is part of any successful business plan, and a great habit to start.

Types of Market Research

Surveys

The simplest way to gather information from your clients or target market is through a survey. You can craft a questionnaire about your product, service, market demographics, buyer motivations, and so on. Anonymous surveys will produce the most accurate information since names are not attached to the results or specific comments.

Depending on the purpose—whether it is to gather demographic information, product or service feedback, or other data—there are a number of ways to administer a survey.

Telephone Surveys

Telephone surveys are a more time-consuming option, but have the benefit of live communication with your target market. Generally, it is best to have a third party conduct this type of survey to gather the most honest feedback. This is the method that market researchers use for polling, which is highly reliable.

Online Surveys

Online surveys are the easiest to administer yourself. There a many web-based services that quickly and easily allow to you custom create your survey, and send it to your email marketing list. These services can also analyse, summarise and interpret the results on your behalf. Keep in mind that the results include only those who are motivated to respond, which may slant your results.

Paper-based Surveys

Paper surveys are seldom used, and can prove to be an inefficient method. Like online surveys, your results are based on the feedback of those who were motivated for one reason or another to respond. However, the time and effort involved in taking the survey, filing it out, and returning it to your place of business may deter people from participating.

Keep in mind that surveys can be complex to administer, and consume more time and resources than you have planned. If you have the budget, consider hiring a professional market research firm to lead or assist with the process. This will also ensure that the methodology is best practice, and will garner the most accurate results.

Website Analysis

Tracking your website traffic is an excellent way to research your existing and potential customer's interests and behaviour. From this information, you can ensure the design, structure and content of your website is catering to the people who use it – and the people you want to use it.

User-friendly website traffic analytics programs can easily show you who is visiting your site, where they are from, and what pages of your site they are viewing. Services like Google Analytics can tell you what page they arrive at, where they click to, how much time they spend on each page, and on which page they leave the site.

This is powerful (and free) information to have in your market research, and easy to monitor monthly or weekly, depending on the needs of your business.

Customer Purchase Data (Consumer Behaviour)

If you do not have the budget to conduct your own professional market research, you can use existing resources on consumer behaviour. While this data may not be specific to your area, general consumer research is actual data that can be helpful in confirming assumptions you may have made about your target market.

Your customer loyalty program or a Point of Sale system may also be of help in tracking customer purchases and identifying trends in purchase behaviour. If you can track who is buying, what they're buying and how often they're buying, you'll have an arsenal of powerful insight into your existing client base.

Focus Groups

Focus groups look at the psychographic and behavioural aspects of your target market. Groups of six to twelve people are gathered and asked general and specific questions about their purchase motivations and behaviour. These questions could relate to your business in particular, or to the general industry.

Focus group sessions can also be time consuming to organise and facilitate, so consider hiring the services of a professional market research firm. You may also receive more honest information if a third party is asking the questions, and receiving the responses from focus group participants.

For cost savings, consider partnering with an organisation in the same industry who is not a direct competitor, and who would benefit from the same market data.

For more valuable business & marketing resources please visit

www.MaximumPerformanceAcademy.com

Or contact the author directly on

info@ MaximumPerformanceAcademy.com

2

HOW TO CREATE A
POWERFUL OFFER

The Crucial Importance of a Powerful Offer

Your offer is the granite foundation of your marketing campaign. Get it right, and everything else will fall into place. Your headline will grab readers, your copy will sing, your advertisement layout will hardly matter, and you will have customers running to your door.

Get it wrong, and even the best looking, best-written campaign will sink like a stone and disappear without a trace.

A powerful offer is an irresistible offer. It's an offer that gets your audience frothing at the mouth and clamouring over each other all the way to your door. An offer that makes your readers pick up the phone and open their wallets.

Irresistible offers make your potential customers think, *'I'd be crazy not to take them up on that'* or *'An offer like this doesn't come around very often!'* They instil a sense of emotion, of desire, and ultimately, urgency.

Make it easy for customers to purchase from you the first time, and spend your time keeping them coming back. Everything else will fall into place once you get your offer right.

The Focus of Your Marketing Campaign

As you work your way through this book, you will find that nearly every chapter discusses the importance of a powerful offer as related to your marketing strategy or promotional campaign.

There's a reason for this.

The powerful offer is more often than not the reason a customer will open their wallets. It is how you generate leads, and then convert them into loyal customers. The more dramatic, unbelievable, and valuable the offer is the more dramatic and unbelievable the response will be.

Many companies spend thousands of pounds on impressive marketing campaigns in glossy magazines and newspapers. They send massive direct mail campaigns on a regular basis; yet don't receive an impressive or massive response rate.

These companies do not yet understand that simply providing information on their company and the benefits of their product is not enough to get customers to act. There is no reason to pick up the phone or visit the store, *right now*.

Your powerful, irresistible offer will:

- Increase leads
- Drive traffic to your website or business
- Move old product
- Convert leads into customers
- Build your customer database

What Makes a Powerful Offer?

A powerful offer is one that makes the most people respond, and take action. It gets people running to spend money on your product or service.

Powerful offers nearly always have an element of *urgency* and of *scarcity*. They give your audience a reason to act immediately, instead of put it off until a later date.

Urgency relates to time

The offer is only available until a certain date, during a certain period of the day, or if you act within a few hours of seeing, or hearing the offer. The customer needs to act now to take advantage of the offer.

Scarcity relates to quantity

There are only a certain number of customers who will be able to take advantage of the offer. There may be a limited number of spaces, a limited number of products, or simply a limited number of people the business will provide the offer to. Again, this requires that customer acts immediately to reap the high value for low cost.

Other Features of Powerful Offers

Offer great value

Customers perceive the offer as having great value – more than a single product on its own, or the product at its regular price. It is clear that the offer takes the customer's needs and wants into consideration.

Make sense to the customer

They are simple and easy to understand if read quickly. Avoid percentages – use half price or 2 for 1 instead of 50% off. There are no catches or requirements, no hoops to jump though and definitely no fine print.

Seem logical

The offer doesn't come out of thin air. There is a logical reason behind it – a holiday, end of season, anniversary celebration, or new product. People can get suspicious of offers that seem too good to be true and have no apparent purpose.

Provide a premium

The offer provides something extra to the customer, like a free gift, or free product or service, so they feel they are getting something extra for no extra cost. Premiums are perceived to have greater value than discounts.

Remember that when your target market reads your offer, they will be asking the following questions:

- What are you offering me?

- What's in it for me?
- What makes me sure I can believe you?
- How much do I have to pay for it?
- Why should I act now?

The Most Powerful Types of Offers

Decide what kind of offer will most effectively achieve your objectives. Are you trying to generate leads, convert customers, build a database, move old product off the shelves, or increase sales?

Consider what type of offer will be of most value to your ideal customers – what offer will make them act quickly.

Free Offer

This type of offer asks customers to act immediately in exchange for something free. This is a good strategy to use to build a customer database or mailing list. Offer a free consultation, free consumer report, or other item of low cost to you but of high perceived value.

You can also advertise the value of the item you are offering for free. For example, act now and you'll receive a free consultation, worth £75. This will dramatically increase your lead generation, and allow you to focus on conversion when the customer comes through the door or picks up the phone.

Package or Bundled Offer

Package your products or services together in a logical way to increase the perceived value as a whole. Discount the value of the package by a small margin, and position it as a start-up kit or special package. By packaging goods of mixed values, you will be able to close more high-value sales. For example: including a free desk-jet printer with every computer purchased.

The Value Added Offer

Add additional services or products that cost you very little, and combine them with other items to increase their attractiveness. This increases the perception of value in the customer's mind, which will justify increasing the price of a product or service without incurring extra hard costs to your business.

Premium Offer

Offer a bonus product or service with the purchase of another. This strategy will serve your bottom line much better than discounting. This includes 2 for 1 offers, offers that include free gifts, and in-store credit with purchases over a specific value.

Urgency Offer

As I mentioned above, offers that include an element of urgency enjoy a better response rate, as there is a reason for your customers to act immediately. Give the offer a deadline or limit the number of spots available.

Guarantee Your Offer by Reversing the Customer's Risk

Offer to take the risk of making a purchase away from your customers. Guarantee the performance or results of your product or service, and offer to compensate the customer with their money back if they are not satisfied. This will help overcome any fear or reservations about your product, and make it more likely for your leads to become customers.

Create Your Powerful Offer

Pick a single product or service

Focus on only one product or service – or one product or service *type* – at a time. This will keep your offer clear, simple, and easy to understand. This can be an area of your business you wish to grow, or old product that you need to move off the shelves.

Decide what you want your customers to do

What are you looking to achieve from your offer? If it is to generate more leads, then you'll need your customer to contact you. If it is to quickly sell old product, you'll need your customer to come into the store and buy it. Do you want them to visit your website? Sign up for your newsletter? How long do they have to act?

Make sure your call to action is clearly stated in your offer.

Dream up the biggest, best offer

First, think of the biggest, best things you could offer your customers – regardless of cost and ability. Don't limit yourself to a single type of offer, combine several types of offers to increase value. Offer a premium, plus a guarantee, with a package offer. Then take a look at what you've created, and make the necessary changes so it is realistic.

Run the numbers

Finally, make sure the offer will leave you with some profit – or at least allow you to break even. You don't want to publish an outrageous offer that will generate a tremendous number of leads, but leave you broke.

Remember that each customer has an acquisition cost, as well as a lifetime value. The amount of their first purchase may allow you to break even, but the amount of their subsequent purchases is where your business will make its profit.

For more valuable business & marketing resources please visit

www.MaximumPerformanceAcademy.com

Or contact the author directly on

info@ MaximumPerformanceAcademy.com

3

HOW TO CREATE EFFECTIVE
MARKETING MATERIALS

Your Marketing Materials Represent Your Business

Your marketing collateral gets sent out in the world to do one thing: to act as an ambassador for your product or service, in place of *you*. This may seem like a big job for a piece of paper, but it's a helpful way to think about the materials you create.

When you meet with a potential or existing client, you do a number of things. You make sure you are well prepared with all the information the customer could need. You dress in clothing that is appropriate. You anticipate their needs, and offer a solution to their problems. You may also like to think about how they prefer to receive information.

Chances are, you wouldn't meet with clients just for the sake of meeting with a client – say, for instance, to show off your new suit. Likewise, you shouldn't create and distribute marketing collateral that is non-essential.

We all know that the biggest challenge for small businesses is the limited number of zeros attached to their marketing budget. Marketing materials can be expensive, and a single, well-produced piece has the ability to devour the entire budget. Given that well-financed marketing campaigns can and do fail on a regular basis, how can you be sure to make the most of, and be successful with, the budget you're working within?

The answer? Limit yourself to only the essential items for your individual business, and produce them *well* with the resources you have.

Your Essential Marketing Materials

The easiest way to throw away your marketing budget is to create and produce marketing materials *you don't need*. Since many pieces of collateral are paper-based, this not only leaves you with boxes of extra (outdated) materials, but also takes a huge toll on the environment.

Take some time to determine what marketing materials you do need, and stick to your list. It's easy to want to *keep up with the Joneses* when your competition comes out with a new piece, but remember your focus should be on attracting and retaining a customer base, not matching the competition item for item.

Know your target market

Make sure you have a solid understanding of your customer base. From that knowledge, you can easily determine what the best way is to reach out and communicate with them. Are they a paper-based or techno savvy client group? Do they appreciate being contacted by email or mail? Are they impressed by flashy design, or simple pieces? *How* you communicate is often just as or more important than *what* you communicate.

Pay attention to costs

Do you really need a die-cut business card? Does your flyer absolutely require ink to the edges? And full colour when perhaps spot colour will do? Unique touches to marketing collateral can grab a customer's attention, but they can also dramatically increase the cost of production. Keep an eye out during the design process and make strategic choices about graphic elements.

Make mistakes – in small batches

Not sure if that flyer is going to do the trick? Test out a limited time offer? Small production runs may cost a little more, but you'll avoid collecting boxes of unusable materials. Or, try a split run with type versions of the same piece and see what works best.

Keep the environment in mind

Environmental responsibility is on everyone's mind these days – including your customers. Always question if a particular marketing item can be produced in electronic format. Consider eliminating plastic bags in exchange for cloth ones, printed with your logo; print everything double-sided; send electronic newsletters; use your website to communicate; and, use recycled paper and envelopes when you can.

Brainstorm your wish list

Create a list of desired marketing materials, and ignore expenses, clients, or any other constraint. Then, beside each item, indicate realistically if it is a needed, wanted, not needed, or electronic item. The next page includes a checklist to get you started. Once you have finished, re-write your list in priority order. This will keep you focused on the essentials only.

Design

The cost of professional design can eat up the majority of your marketing budget in a hurry. However, the cost of distributing materials that look and feel unprofessional can often be much higher. The key is to find the middle ground.

Unless you have design or desktop publishing experience – or even if you do – your time is probably not best spent designing your own marketing materials. Depending on the size of your business and your graphic needs (i.e., Do you need frequent photography of your products?) there are a number of options you can choose from:

Hire a design agency

This is no doubt the most costly of your options. However, if you have a number of items to be designed, you may be able to get a package rate. Another option is to have the design agency create a logo and stationery package for you, then create a style guide for use of the logo, fonts, and other graphic elements in the rest of your marketing materials.

Hire a freelance designer

For most small businesses, the benefits of using a freelance designer (aside from cost savings) are convenience and trust. If you are lucky enough to find one you work well with, work hard to establish a seamless working relationship and you'll never worry about the design of your marketing materials again. Ask associates for recommendations of local designers, or consider posting an advertisement on one of the online directories.

Hire a part-time design employee

Need to hire someone part-time for a task around the office or shop? Consider recruiting someone with design skills and hiring them for full-time work. This could include graphic design students, or someone with an interest and talent in the field.

Whichever option you choose – or if you choose to design your materials yourself - the two most important things to remember about design are:

Keep it consistent

Your marketing materials must be consistent, or your customers will never learn to recognise your brand

Keep it simple

Simple, clean design is the most effective way of communicating. Use *'wow'* pieces sparingly.

Marketing Materials Checklist

Item	Need	Want	Don't Need	Digital
Logo				
Business Cards				
Brochure				
Website				
Newsletter				
Catalogue				
Advertisements				
Flyers				
Branded Items e.g. pens, seasonal gifts				
Employee Clothing				
Product Labels				
External / Vehicle Signage				
Internal Document Templates				
Email Signature				
Blog				
Letterhead + Envelopes				
Notepads				
Company Profile				

Headlines & Sub-headlines

If your headlines were the only thing that a potential customer reads, how do you think your marketing materials would fare? Headlines need to be bold, dramatic, shocking and absolutely answer the questions *'What's in it for me?'* or, *'Why should I care?'*

Headlines (and sub-headlines) are vital in today's market because we are bombarded with so much information that we scan everything. Readers are skimming your materials to find out why they should bother paying attention to your product or service. Hit their hot buttons, and tell them why they should care, in your headlines!

Remember that headlines and sub-headlines are not just for advertisements. They work wonders in newsletters, sales letters, brochures and websites, and can be incorporated into all of your essential marketing materials.

Guidelines for the Top 10 Marketing Materials

Logo

Use design resources
If you are going to spend any money on outside design help, this is the time to do it. Your logo is the visual representation of your product or service, and appears on everything that relates to your business. This is the core of your brand image, and needs to be done right the first time.

Remember the purpose

The logo needs to be a unique reflection of your business, your business values, and the industry you work in. Before you commit to your logo, make sure to give careful consideration to colour choice, image selection and image recognition – as well as the logos that already exist in the marketplace. Test it out on your family and friends for an outside opinion and use their feedback.

Don't get too complicated

Can it be produced (and seen clearly) in black and white? In a single colour? With your company name? Too often businesses design their own logos that include a complex assortment of photos, words, and solid design elements. These do not photocopy well, and can't be clearly read at a small scale. Keep your logo design down to a graphic image and the name of your business.

Business Cards

Cover the basics

A business card needs to communicate your basic contact information to potential clients, including who you are and what your business does. Make sure you've covered the basics and made it easy for them to be in touch.

- Name
- Job Title
- Your Email Address
- Your Mobile Number (if applicable)
- Company Name

- Company Slogan / Description
- Company Phone Number
- Company Fax Number
- Company Address (if appropriate)
- Website address
- QR code linking to your website or online offer
- Use both sides of the card

Make it memorable; be creative

Choose interesting shapes and sizes (square, folded or post-card sized), die-cuts, orientation (vertical vs. horizontal), bright colours, and unique materials (wood, plastic, magnet, aluminium or foam). You don't have to go crazy or spend lots of money to do this – simple, clever twists on basic design make an impact. Just keep it relevant to your product or service.

Give your customers a reason to keep it

What is going to stop a customer from throwing it out, or filing it in a binder with other business cards? Make the card worth keeping by adding something useful to the reverse. For example, coffee shops put frequent buyer incentives on the reverse of their cards, encouraging customers to keep them in their wallets. Other examples include pick-up schedules, reminders, calendars, quotations, testimonials, or coupons.

Produce a high quality business card

Use a quality card stock and print in colour. Choose clear, easy to read fonts that aren't any smaller than 9pt and avoid white letters on a dark background which is hard to read. Ask your designer about printing techniques that might make your card stand out and consider using your photograph.

Use your business card as a lead generation device

Give people a reason to call you, log on to your website or request further information. Even if they don't need your services immediately, if you can capture their email address you can keep in touch with them so that you'll be top of mind if they should need your services in the future.

Letterhead

Ensure a professional quality

A letterhead that is simple, clean, and well produced allows the reader to focus on the important part: the content. Have your letterhead professionally printed on quality paper, or choose a textured stock. Show that you have invested in the professionalism of your company.

Pay attention to design choices

The design of your marketing collateral should reflect your corporate values and the personality of your organisation. If you are environmentally conscious, choose recycled paper and write it in small print at the bottom of the page. Your letterhead can also be a place for subtle graphic elements, like watermarks, in addition to your logo.

Keep consistent with other materials

Your letterhead is part of your stationery package, and should look and feel the same as the rest of your pieces. For example, if your business cards have been printed with rounded corners, so should your letterhead. Use consistent fonts, colours, and logo placement on your letterhead, business cards, fax cover sheets, and other internal documents to ensure recognition and ease of readability.

Brochures

Cover the basics

Each brochure you produce should include your basic marketing message, your Unique Selling Proposition, and company contact information. Product or service features, and customer benefits should be clearly displayed and described.

Be purpose-focused

Why are you producing this brochure? Are you featuring a new product line? Trying to increase awareness? Introducing your service to a new market? Stay closely connected to the purpose behind your brochure, and ensure that all of the information and images in the brochure support that purpose.

Keep it simple

Make sure the design and layout is clean and easy to navigate. Like advertisements, leaving blank spaces gives the reader a break and makes it easier for them to notice your key messages.

Choose high quality production

If you don't invest in your business, why should anyone else? Produce your brochure on high quality paper, in vivid colour, and have it professionally folded. An impressive-looking brochure will travel farther than a homemade one – from the hand of one client to another.

Downloadable brochures

If you are producing your brochure electronically, as a download from your website or for emailing to customers, invest in design as you would for a printed brochure. Your customers will notice the difference.

Keep brochures up-to-date

If you produce brochures on a regular basis, consider giving each a theme to distinguish the information as new and interesting. Keep the overall look and feel consistent, but play with images and content layout to revitalise the design.

Newsletters

Keep in touch

Don't wait until your existing clients walk back into your store. Show them that they are important to your business, and keep them updated on new products and services by keeping distributing a personalised newsletter.

Use an online distribution service

Online email marketing tools (CRM tools) have never been easier or cheaper to use, and enable you to personalise your letters without too much effort. They will also track for you which clients open their newsletters, and which click through to your website.

Provide information; tell a story

Engage the reader with a short anecdote, or a piece of relevant information. People are bombarded by email newsletters on a daily basis, so make sure yours is worthy of their reading time. Include an *Ask the Expert* or *New Products* section and structure the newsletter like your own business newspaper. Add links, or references to relevant media articles, or special offers.

Choose a frequency you can maintain

Newsletters can be time consuming, so be realistic about how often you promise to distribute them. This depends on your resources, and the needs of your business, but generally once a month to once every three months is a good time frame.

Company Profile

Your ultimate company brochure

Your company profile includes all important information on your business and your offerings, and acts as the base for all other marketing items. These are generally longer pieces – from five to 20 pages in length, allowing you ample room for written and visual content.

Tell your story

The company profile is the place to tell the story of your business. Engage the reader, use anecdotes, and describe how and why your company was created. If you inherited the family business, describe how you're carrying on tradition and instilling new life. If you created your company from scratch with friends from University, let the reader know. These real life details are interesting and establish trust with your potential clients and associates, but keep it succinct and to the point.

Communicate your values

Here you have the space to describe your company's vision, values and approach, or philosophies. Make sure you relate your values to your offering, and, like the previous section, keep this section short and succinct.

Explain your offering – concentrating on the benefits

Just like your brochure, make sure to describe the full benefits that your customers enjoy from your product or service. Use testimonials throughout to back up your statements. This can include your full range of services, or simply an overview of your product types. Use professional images and creative copy to keep readers engaged.

Choose high-quality design and production

Spend time creating a company profile that will last. Then, spend money producing one that will impress. Choose glossy paper, and a high-quality printer, and leave the profiles around your store and office for clients to read and admire.

Signage

Get professional advice

Outdoor signage can be a daunting task for anyone who hasn't designed, produced, or otherwise gone through the process. Since signage is influenced by a variety of factors – one of which is local authority rules and regulations – you may wish to enlist the help of a professional (a signage designer or printer) to guide you through the process and avoid costly errors.

Make it visible

All of your outdoor signage should be easily seen from the street, or within the location in which you are situated. In some cases, you may need more than one sign to do this. Keep in mind how your sign will look at night, as well as during the day, as your company logo and phone number or website needs to be visible at all times.

Make it distinct

When it comes to signage, you can get really creative with materials, lights, and colours. While you need to maintain consistency with your other materials, you can add other graphic elements that may not work on the rest of your collateral, including 3D elements and window treatments. Make it memorable and eye-catching if possible.

Vehicle signage

Sign-written vehicles are a sign that you are serious about your business. Whether you are a start-up hypnotherapist, an estate agent or a florist, a sign-written vehicle costs about the same as a single advertisement in the local paper, but lasts much, much longer.

Remember your indoor signage

Many businesses need indoor signage to continually remind customers where they are. This includes section signage, product signage, way-finding systems, and promotion announcements. If your business is located in an office, consider signage with your logo and company name above the reception area. Again, keep this signage consistent with the rest of your company materials, and you will be contributing to brand recognition.

Advertisements & Flyers

Place advertisements strategically

Once you have determined your target market, you need to focus on advertising in the publications they are most likely to read, and distributing flyers in places they are most likely to be. Spend strategically. Take time to test which publications work best by measuring the response from each placement. And, when you place print advertisements, insist that they are placed in the first half of the publication and on a right hand page, preferably at the top.

Grab your customer's attention

You have less than half a second to grab the attention of your audience with print advertising, so use it wisely. Spend the bulk of your time crafting the headline and choosing compelling images.

Keep your customer's attention

If you caught their attention, you have another two seconds to keep it. Use sub-headings to further entice them to read on for the details of your product or service offer.

Tell your customers why they should buy

Always include your marketing message or USP in your advertising. Describe the features and benefits of your product or service, but focus on the benefits that will trigger an emotional response from your target audience – love, money, luxury, convenience, and security.

Tell your customers how they can buy

Include a call to action beside your contact information, and include your phone number, website address, and business address (if applicable). You may wish to include a scarcity or urgency offer to compel your readers to act fast.

Know the importance of white space

If you try to cram too much information into your advertisement or flyer, your readers will skip it. Clean, clear, easy to read ads and one-page flyers with succinct messages are most effective.

Website

Be purpose-focused

Like your brochure, your website can serve a number of purposes. To be effective, you need to narrow in on the specific purpose when designing the content structure of the pages. Who is your audience? What do you want them to leave the site knowing? What do you want the site to make them do? Visit your store? Buy your offering? Pick up the phone? Make sure you are clear on this point before you start.

Make the address easy to remember

A website address that is too long or too complicated will not get remembered, or found. Search for available website addresses that relate to your business or marketing message, and try to secure a site with a .co.uk or .com ending. If your company name is taken, use your USP or guarantee instead.

Focus on content

The overall structure of how you organise the content on your site is like the foundation of your house. You can change the paint colour, and the furniture, but the foundation is more or less there for good. Before you work with a designer and create the visual fabric of your website, focus on creating solid copy that is clearly organised. Put together a site map of your website structure, starting with your homepage and sub-pages, and allocating specific content to each page.

Add new content regularly

Your company is always changing, and so should your website. This is an important (and relatively inexpensive) way to communicate your company news and achievements, and most likely the easiest accessed source of information. Have areas for easy content updates – like a *news* section – and make sure sections like *employees* and *services* are kept up to date. For larger updates, go back to your purpose and website map, and make sure the content changes still support the original intent of the website.

Make your website easy to use

Make key information easy to access, especially your contact information. You can quickly tell if a website is easy to navigate, because the information you are looking for appears in a natural order. For example, when visiting a restaurant website, a link to the reservations page is provided on the menu page. While you're putting together your website map, do some research online and investigate what does and doesn't work. A good rule of thumb is to ensure it takes no more than three clicks to access a page. Bury content too deep, and your audience will get frustrated and leave.

Keep consistent with marketing materials

Your website is an extension of your marketing campaign, and should be treated as such. Use consistent logo placements, fonts, colours and images so that all elements of your collateral are unified. Likewise with marketing campaigns. If you are running a new promotion, or featuring a new item in an advertisement, include that information on your website. Customers responding to the advertisement will be reinforced, and customers who did not see the advertisement will be aware of the offer.

Measure your results

Your website is a piece of your marketing collateral, just like brochures and advertisements, and should be evaluated for effectiveness on a regular basis. Easy website analysis tools, like Google Analytics, will show you which pages your audience is viewing, how long they're staying on each page, and where and when they leave the site. That is powerful information when it comes to structuring content, and choosing which page to put your most important messages.

Most important

Email marketing is still a cost-effective method to keep your products and services top of mind in your customers. So use your website to capture the email addresses of visitors so that you can keep in touch with them.

For more valuable business & marketing resources please visit

www.MaximumPerformanceAcademy.com

Or contact the author directly on

info@ MaximumPerformanceAcademy.com

4

HOW TO USE TESTIMONIALS & PROFIT FROM SOCIAL PROOF

The Power of Testimonials

Testimonials are simply the single most powerful asset you can have in your marketing toolkit. When your customers tell others about the benefits of choosing your business, it is a thousand times more powerful than the same words from your mouth.

The words and opinions of others motivate people to spend money every day. From celebrity endorsements on TV and in magazines, to casual conversations with friends, decisions about what product or service to buy – and what brand or provider – are heavily influenced by those who have purchased before.

Why? There are several reasons. Many people have an inherent distrust of salespeople, and a scepticism toward marketing materials. Others are bombarded with choice, and are looking for some sense of security in their purchase decision.

Testimonials build the credibility of your business, break down natural barriers, and create a sense of trust for the customer. They have an incredible ability to persuade customers to buy, and to buy from you. Think about the last time someone recommended a brand of laundry detergent, a bottle of wine, or a plumber to you. Their positive experience had more of an impact on your decision to buy than any advertisement or discount.

When it comes to spending money, people want to feel safe. They want to know that someone else has bought before, and they want to know that the product or service has delivered the promised results. A testimonial for your business is worth more than any advertising copy clever slogan, or sales pitch.

Customers Who Give Testimonials

When people put their name and reputation on paper to endorse something, it creates a sense of loyalty and if questioned, they will cheerfully justify their decision.

When someone is willing to endorse your product or service in writing, they have likely already started a word-of-mouth chain of verbal testimonials about their positive experience. Remember the last time you discovered a chiropractic miracle worker? Or the fastest and cheapest drycleaner? Didn't you tell every one of your friends who could use the service?

By asking a customer for a testimonial, you are asking for their assistance in the growth of your business. When they feel they are truly helping and participating in the development of your company, their sense of pride will mean continuous loyalty to your product or service.

11 Ways to Get Great Testimonials

Testimonials are powerful – no question. But how do you make sure that the words you get from your customers will bring you the most value? How do you ensure that your client will articulate your product's merits in a clear and easy to understand way? How do you make sure you can actually use their testimonials in your marketing materials?

Asking for testimonials requires more effort than merely soliciting general comments and praise. You want to ensure that your customer feels a sense of pride and loyalty in providing their opinion, and that their opinion will have an impact on potential buyers.

Here are 11 proven ways to get great testimonials from your customers.

1. Strike while the iron is hot!
Your customers are the happiest and most willing to help you within a day to a week of their purchase, so aim to secure the testimonial in this time period. Ask for the testimonial before they leave, and make sure you have all their contact details to follow up with. This also ensures you stay on top of your testimonial recruitment!

2. Be specific

Specific testimonials are more believable. The more specific you can have your customer be, the stronger and more impactful the testimonial will be. Meaningful details get remembered. Ask for mention of things like time, dates, extraordinary customer service, and personal observations.

3. If you were the solution – what was the problem?

Testimonials that tell stories are more engaging. Ask client to not only describe their experience with your company, but also the negative experience that led them to your door. If they can describe the struggles and challenges they were facing before receiving your service, the reader will likely be able to sympathise and resonate with similar struggles. This will motivate them to solve their problems with your solution.

4. Write the first draft for them

Make it easy for your clients. This technique is something you can offer someone who is hesitant to commit to writing a testimonial due to time constraints, or is procrastinating. Ask them to brainstorm a few notes they would like to include in their feedback, write them down, and string them into a concise testimonial for their review. All they have to do is review, print on their letterhead, sign, and mail back to you!

5. Include your marketing message or USP

Always ask your customers to include your unique selling proposition (USP) in the testimonial. For instance, if your USP includes exceptional customer service, same-day installation, and a money-back guarantee then ask your customer to mention some of those qualities in their testimonial.

6. A picture says...

Yes, you know the saying, and it's true. When readers attach an image of the speaker to words, the words are enlivened and have twice as much validity and impact. When readers see an image of a previous client using your product or service, their words and opinions are even more believable. You can take these simple pictures yourself – and take many so you have a selection to choose from – or use stock photos of happy smiling customers.

7. Credentials equal trust

As we mentioned, testimonials from credible sources will have the most believability and impact. When you ask for a testimonial, make sure your customer states their expertise and credentials. If you sell custom orthotics, and can secure a solid testimonial from a doctor, their words will be golden in your marketing materials.

8. Don't forget to ask permission

When you ask for testimonials, make sure you are clear that their words may be used in your marketing materials, including advertisements, website and in-store displays. This is a good time to thank them for their time and sincerity, and show your appreciation for their words.

9. Location, location...

Depending on the market reach of your business, the location of your customers is an important part of the believability of your testimonial. If you own a community-based business, when potential clients see you've made others happy just down their street they'll be motivated to use your service too. If you own a regional business, then the cities and addresses of other happy customers can help communicate the reach of your service.

10. Testimonials are not surveys

Keep the purpose of your request in mind when you're asking for testimonials. Testimonials should provide positive material for your advertising materials. Surveys are used to solicit meaningful (and often confidential) customer information to refine and improve your service. Testimonials are public statements, while surveys are often anonymous and can produce less-than-positive results.

11. Say 'Thank You!'

Thanking a customer for their time and effort creating your testimonial is just plain good manners. It also increases loyalty and goodwill. This can be done via email, but sending a letter on your letterhead is a more personal approach that will be more meaningful to the recipient.

Using Testimonials Strategically

So now you have a pile of glowing customer testimonials. What's next?

Choose the most powerful piece of the testimonial

What is the most convincing aspect of the testimonial? Is it the author? Where they are from? A specific sentence or paragraph they wrote? Be strategic about the aspect of the testimonial that you feature, and select what will have the most impact.

You can compile a list titled *What Customers are Saying*, and list only the phrases that best support your specific marketing message. Or you can feature the unique credentials or story of your customer, before you even include their testimonial. You can also summarise the testimonial with a powerful headline.

Put them on your website

Adding a page of testimonials to your website is a great start, especially when you're beginning to solicit customer responses. However, the most powerful way to ensure site visitors actually see your testimonials is to include them on every page – especially the ones with the highest traffic.

A testimonial should be placed wherever you make a strong statement about your service or product, and wherever the service or product is described. This is a great way to break up your sales copy with some social proof. As your visitors read about your offering, your credibility will be validated by someone other than you.

Compile your best 25 to 50 letters in a display book

Keep a book of testimonials in the waiting area of your office, your boardroom, and in your desk. Or, put one at the service counter, cash register and anywhere else people may have a moment to flip through.

You can do this if you're a recruiting firm, a hardware store, or a chiropractor. When clients have a chance to read the positive experiences of others, they will be more open to hearing your sales pitch less guarded when responding to your unique offering.

Hang your favourite testimonials in your store or office

Testimonials as art! Frame your favourite testimonials – preferably the ones written on client letterhead – and post them on the wall in your business. Even if clients don't read them up close, the volume and visual recognition of client logos will have impact. Plus – your next satisfied clients will want to see their company names on the wall too.

Put them in your advertisements

Use short, clear, concise testimonials in your advertising. The best advertisers know that testimonials are the fastest and most effective way to overcome scepticism and get clients thinking that your product or service is the solution to their problem.

Include a page of testimonials in your direct mail

When sending your marketing materials directly to a mass list of potential clients, let the words of others speak to the merits of your product or service. Put together a page or two of testimonials, and attach it to your mailing. The credibility of your company will be instantly established, encouraging clients to act – and buy – faster.

Testimonial Examples

Below you will find a series of sample testimonials, and excerpts from testimonial letters. Read these over, and take a moment to notice why each is a powerful statement. We have also summarised each testimonial with a headline and don't forget, your testimonials will normally include your customer's name and company.

24% Response Rate from a Single Direct Mailing!

We were sceptical about direct mail campaigns, and unsure about the return on investment. Your strategic advice and logistical help made the project run smoothly and easily – we received over 200 leads from this single effort!

Best Sleep in 20 Years!

I can't tell you how much I appreciated Craig's patience and assistance in my mattress selection. He is so knowledgeable about the design and features of each mattress, and helped us find a financing solution that worked with our budget. I haven't slept this well in over two decades. Promote him!

A Gentle & Effective Approach

I have always been reluctant to visit a chiropractor for my lower back pain because I am not comfortable with physical adjustments. Sarah took the time to clearly explain the cause of my pain, and gave me easy exercises to help correct the problem. She respected my comfort level, and treated me without uncomfortable cracks and snaps!

Testimonial Request Letter

Here is an example of a basic testimonial request letter that can be customised and made into a template for your business. This can also be sent by email if that is how your clients prefer to be contacted.

Mr. John Smith
Company Name
123 Main Street

1 January, 20XX

Dear Mr. Smith,

Thank you for visiting our store this week. It was a pleasure helping you select a new laptop for your daughter to use at university – they just grow up too fast! Your research and clear idea of the product you were searching for made our job easy.

We know there are a lot of choices when it comes to purchasing a laptop, so thank you for choosing us. If there is anything else we can assist you with, please don't hesitate to contact me directly.

We occasionally ask select customers for their feedback in the form of a testimonial. Because we are so proud of the feedback we receive, we often use our customer's quotes in our marketing materials – specifically our website and sales brochures. The real life experiences of our customers are stories that we are proud of.

Could I ask you to write down some of your feedback, please? A few words about your experience, and how we helped you and your daughter would be greatly appreciated. We encourage you to print this on your company letterhead, so we can provide your own company with some exposure as well.

You may want to include the names of the members of staff who helped you, and how your daughter is enjoying her laptop. Again, we would like to feature your name and experience in our marketing materials. For your convenience, I've included a prepaid envelope with which to mail your testimonial back to us.

Thank you very much for your assistance.

Kind regards,

Your name here

Testimonial Thank You Letter

Here is an example of a short thank you letter for a testimonial that can also be customised and made into a template for your unique business. You may wish to use cards for your thank you letters, but try to avoid sending thank you letters via email.

Mr. John Smith

1 January, 20XX

Dear Mr. Smith,

We received your glowing testimonial in the mail today, and I wanted to thank you personally for your kind words. Your comments about our store and our people are important to us, and I will make sure the staff take a moment to read your letter.

We are thrilled that your daughter is enjoying her laptop, and using it to keep in touch with you while she studies abroad. When we sold it to you, we truly believed it would provide the most long-lasting value for her student budget. I hope it serves her for the rest of her time at school.

Thank you again for taking the time to write us. We are all proud to have been of service to you and your daughter, and look forward to seeing you both again soon.

Kind regards,

Your Name Here

Testimonial Worksheet

Name Phone & Email	Request Letter Sent	Follow Up Call Made	Testimonial Received	Thank-you Letter Sent
	☐	☐	☐	☐
	☐	☐	☐	☐
	☐	☐	☐	☐
	☐	☐	☐	☐
	☐	☐	☐	☐
	☐	☐	☐	☐
	☐	☐	☐	☐
	☐	☐	☐	☐

Create a Testimonial Worksheet

Brainstorm a list of recent customers and clients who you will approach for testimonials. Post this worksheet in your office, and track your progress. You can never have too many so aim for 50 testimonials in two months and then keep renewing them on a regular basis.

Start today!

For more valuable business & marketing resources please visit

www.MaximumPerformanceAcademy.com

or contact the author directly on

info@ MaximumPerformanceAcademy.com

5

HOW TO CREATE
IMMEDIATE SALES

If You're in Business, You're in Sales!

If you're a business owner, you're also a salesperson.

You've had to sell to the bank to get them to loan you your start-up capital. You've had to sell to your best employees on why they should work for your business. You've had to convince your business partner, spouse, and friends why your business idea is a good one.

Now you have to repeatedly sell your product or service to your customers.

The ability to sell effectively and efficiently is one every successful business owner has cultivated, and continues to develop. It can be a complicated and time consuming task; one that you will have to continually work on throughout your career in order to be – and stay – successful.

Fortunately, making sales is a step-by-step process that can be learned, customised, and continuously improved. There are a wide range of tools available to help and support your sales efforts.

You don't have to be the most outgoing, enthusiastic person to be successful at sales. You don't even have to be a good public speaker. All you need is an understanding of the basic sales process, and a genuine passion for what you are selling.

Sales 101

Making sales is a process. There are clear, step-by-step actions that can be taken and result in a sale.

The sales process varies according to the type of business, type of customers and type of product or service that is offered; however, the core steps are the same. Similarly, sales training varies from individual to individual, but the core skills and abilities remain the same.

Here is a basic seven-step process that you can follow, or fine tune to suit your unique products and services. Remember that each step is important, and builds on the step previous. It is essential to become adept at each step, instead of solely focusing on closing the sale.

1. Preparation
2. Build a relationship

3. Discuss needs & wants
4. Present the solution
5. Overcome objections
6. Close
7. Service & follow up

Points 3, 4 & 5 are presented in a sequence. In reality, unless your sales is straightforward and can be accomplished in one interaction, this part of the sales process can be quite drawn out as different solutions are presented, and unexpected requirements and objections surface.

You will find closing comes naturally if you have done everything else correctly and your product / service matches your customer's needs and it is within their budget.

1. Preparation

Make sure you have prepared for your meeting, presentation, or day on the sales floor. You have complete control of this part of the sales process, so it is important to do everything you can to set the stage for your success.

- Understand your product or service inside and out
- Prepare all the necessary materials, and be organised
- Keep your place of business tidy
- Ensure you appear professional and well groomed
- Do some research on your potential client and brainstorm to find common ground

2. Build a Relationship

The first few minutes you spend with a potential customer set the stage for the rest of your interaction. First impressions are everything. Your goal in the second step is to relax the customer and begin to develop a relationship with them. Establishing a real relationship with your customer will create trust.

- Make a great first impression: shake hands, make eye contact, and introduce yourself
- Remain confident and professional, but also personable
- Mirror their speech and behaviour
- Begin with general questions and small talk
- Show interest in them and their place of business
- Notice and comment on positives
- Find some common ground on which to relate

3. Discuss Needs & Wants

Once you have spent a few moments getting to know your prospect, start asking open-ended questions to discover some of their needs and wants.

If they have come to you on the sales floor, ask what brought them into the store. If you are meeting them to present your product or service, ask why they are interested in it, or what criteria they have in mind for that product or service.

If you are making a sales presentation, ask for a few moments at the outset to outline the purpose of your visit, as well as to explain how you have structured the presentation

- Listen intently, and repeat back information you are not sure you understand
- Ask open-ended questions to get them talking. The longer they talk, the more insight they are providing you into their needs and purchase motivations
- Ask clarifying questions about their responses
- If you become sure the customer is going to buy your product or service, begin to ask more specific questions about what it is that you are offering and how they see themselves benefiting from using the product or service

Make sure you establish the decision making process and any budgetary expectations. No point in presenting your £10,000 solution if the budget is £1,000. Likewise, if your solution is £10,000 and their budget is £100,000 it's highly likely that you will have missed something.

4. Present the Solution
Once you have a solid understanding of what they are looking for, or what issue they are looking to resolve, you can begin to present the solution: your product or service.

- Explain how your product or service will solve their problem or meeting their needs. If several products apply, begin by presenting the mid-level product
- Illustrate your points with anecdotes about other happy customers, or awards the product or service has earned
- Use hypothetical examples featuring your customer and encourage them to picture a scenario after their purchase

- Begin by describing the benefits of the product, then follow up with features and advantages
- Watch your customer's behaviour as you speak, and ask further qualifying questions in response to body language and verbal comments
- Give the customer an opportunity to ask you questions or provide feedback about each product or service after you have described or explained it
- Ask closed-ended questions to confirm points made and obtain agreement

5. Overcome Objections

As you present the product or service, take note of potential objections by asking open-ended questions and monitoring body language. Expect that objections will arise and prepare for them. Consider brainstorming a list of all potential objections, and writing down your responses.

- Repeat the objection back to the customer to ensure you understand them correctly
- Empathise with what they have said, and then provide a response that overcomes the objection
- Confirm that the answer you have provided has overcome their objection by repeating yourself

The 8 Most Common Objections

- The product or service does not seem valuable to me
- There is no reason for me to act know so I will wait
- It's safest not to make a decision right away

- There is not enough money for the purchase
- The competitor or another department offers a better product
- There are internal issues between people or departments
- The relationship with the decision maker is strained
- There is an existing contract in place with another business

6. Close

This is an important part of the sales process that should be handled delicately. Deciding when to close is a judgment call that must be made in the moment during the sale.

Ideally, if you have presented a solution to their problem and overcome any objections, you will have the customer in a place where they are ready to buy.

Here are some questions to ask before you close the sale:

- Does my customer agree that there is value in my product or service?
- Does my customer understand the features and benefits of the product or service?
- Are there any remaining objections that must be handled?
- What other factors could influence my customer's decision to buy?
- Have I minimised the customer's risk involved in making the purchase, and provided some level of urgency?

Once you have determined it is time to make the sale, here are some sample statements you can use to get the process rolling:

- So, should we get started?
- Shall I grab a new one from the back?
- If you just give me your credit card, I can take care of the transaction while you continue browsing.
- When would you like the product delivered?
- We can begin next month if we receive payment by the end of the week.
- Can I email you a draft contract tomorrow?

7. Service & Follow-up

Once you have made the sale, your work is not over. You want to ensure that that customer will become a loyal, repeat customer, and that they will refer their friends to your business.

Ask them to be in your customer database, and keep in touch with regular newsletters. Follow up with a phone call or drop by to ask how they are enjoying the product or service, and if they have any further questions or needs you can assist them with.

This contact opportunity will also allow you to ask for a referral, or an up-sell. At the very least, it will ensure you are continuing to foster and build a relationship with the client.

Up-selling & Cross-selling

Up-selling is simply inviting your customers to spend more money in your business by purchasing additional products or services. This could include more of the same product, complementary products, or impulse items.

Up-selling, and its close relative Cross-selling are effective ways to increase profits and create loyal clients – without spending any money to acquire the business. These clients are already purchasing from you – which means they perceive value in what you have to offer – so take the information you have gained in the sales process and offer them a little bit more.

You experience up selling on a daily basis. From *'Do you want fries with that?'* to *'Have you heard about our product protection plan?'* Companies across the globe have tapped into and trained their staff on the value of the up sell.

Ethical up-selling is rooted in good customer service. If your client purchases a new computer printer, you'll need to make sure they have the cables they need to connect it to the computer, regular and photo paper, ink cartridges and so on.

If you don't suggest these items, they may arrive home and realise they do not have all the materials needed to use the product. They may choose to purchase those materials somewhere closer, cheaper, or more helpful.

Customer education is another form of up-selling. What if your customer doesn't realise that you sell a variety of printer paper and stationery in addition to computer hardware like printers? Take every opportunity to educate your customer on the products and services you offer that may be of interest to them.

An effective way of implementing an up sell system into your business is simply by creating add-on checklists for the products or services you offer. Each item has a list of related items that your customer may need. This will encourage your staff to develop the habit of asking for the up sell.

Up-selling strategies can be implemented:

At the point of sale
This is a great place for impulse items like confectionary, torch batteries, etc.

In a newsletter
This is an effective strategy for customer education

In your merchandising
Place strips of impulse items near related items. For example, paper clips with paper and pens near binders

Over the phone
If someone is placing an order for delivery, offer additional items in the same shipment for convenience

With new products
Feature each new product or service that you offer prominently in your business, and ask your staff to mention it to every customer

Sales Team

Employing a team of strong salespeople is one of the best ways to ensure the long term success of your business.

What Makes a Good Salesperson?

There are a lot of salespeople out there – but what qualities and skills make a great salesperson?

These are the attributes you will want to find or develop in your team:

- Willingness to continuously learn and improve sales skills
- Sincerity in relating to customers and providing solutions to their objectives
- An understanding of the company's big picture
- A communication style that is direct, polite, and professional
- Honesty and respect for other team members, customers, as well as the competition.
- Ability to manage time & be well organised
- Enthusiastic
- Inquisitive
- A great listener
- Ability to quickly interpret, analyse, and respond to information during the sales process
- Ability to connect and develop relationships of trust with potential clients
- Professional appearance

Team Building – Keeping Your Team Together

In many businesses, sales is a department or a whole team of people who work together to generate leads and convert customers. Effective management of your sales team is a skill every business owner should cultivate.

Communication

- Are targets and results regularly reviewed?
- Are opportunities for input regularly provided?
- Do sales staff members have a clear understanding of what is expected?
- Do all staff members know daily, weekly, and quarterly targets?

Performance Management

- Are sales staff members motivated to reach targets?
- Are sales staff recognised and rewarded once those targets are reached?
- Are there opportunities for skills training and development?
- Do staff members have broad and comprehensive product or industry knowledge?
- Is there opportunity for growth within the company?
- Is performance regularly reviewed?

Operations

- Do you have a solid understanding of your sales numbers (revenue, profit, margins)?
- Are your sales processes regularly reviewed?
- Do you have a variety of sales scripts prepared?
- Do you measure conversion rates?
- How are your leads generated?

Sales Tools

Every salesperson should have the tools they need on hand to assist them in the sales process. These tools can act as aids while a sale is taking place, or help to foster continual learning and development of the salesperson's skills and approach.

The list opposite includes some popular sales tools. Add to this list with other resources that are specific to your business or industry.

Sales Tool	Description & Benefit
Scripts	- Used for incoming and outgoing telemarketing, cold calls, door-to-door sales, in-store sales - Create several different scripts for your business - Maintains consistency in your sales approach - Revise and renew your scripts regularly
Presentation Materials	- High-quality information about your offerings - Forms: brochure, product sheets, proposals - PowerPoint presentations can serve as an outline of your sales presentation and keep you on track
Colleagues	- A source of help and advice, especially when you are on the same team or sell similar products - Also a source of support
Customer Databases	- An accurate, up-to-date database of customer contact information and contact history - Used to stay in touch with clients - Can also be used for direct mail and follow-up telemarketing
The Internet	- A powerful resource for sales help and advice - Information to help improve your sales process - Online sales coaching - Source of product knowledge
Ongoing Training	- Constant improvement of your sales skills - Constant increase in product knowledge - Investment in yourself and your company

8 Tips for Better Sales Results (+ 1 Bonus Tip)

Tip 1: Dress for success

Dress professionally, appear well put together and maintain good hygiene. Ensure you are not only dressed professionally, but *appropriately*. Would your client feel more comfortable if you wore a suit, or jeans and blazer?

Tip 2: Speak their language

Show you understand their industry or culture, and use phrases your customer understands. This may require researching industry jargon or common phrases. Remember to avoid using words and phrases that are used in the sales process: sold, contract, telemarketing, finance, interest, etc. Doing so will help break down the salesperson/customer barrier.

Tip 3: Always be positive

Show up or answer the phone with a smile, and leave your personal or business issues behind. Be enthusiastic about what you have to offer, and how that offering will benefit your customer. Reflect this not only in your voice, but also in your body language.

Tip 4: Deliver a strong pitch or presentation

Be confident and convincing. Leave self-doubt at the door, and walk in assuming the sale. Take time to explain complex concepts, and always connect what you're saying to your audience in a specific way.

Tip 5: Exhibit good manners to everyone at all times

Accept any amenity you're offered, listen intently, don't interrupt, be on time, have a strong handshake, look people in the eye when you speak with them and give everyone you are speaking to equal attention. This is so important that I'd say, if good manners don't come naturally to you, steer clear of sales.

Tip 6: Avoid sensitive subjects

Politics, religion, swearing, sexual innuendos and racial comments are strictly off-limits. So are negative comments about other customers or the competition. I can be confident that none of my customers have ever heard me swear – because I never do!

Tip 7: Create a real relationship & know how to develop rapport

Icebreakers and small talk are not just to pass the time before your presentation. They are how relationships get established. Show genuine interest in everything your customer has to say. Ask questions about topics you know they are passionate about. Speak person to person, not salesperson to customer. Remember everything.

Tip 8: Know more than you need to

Impress clients with comprehensive knowledge – not only of your product or service – but also of the people who use that product or service, and industry trends. Be seen as an expert in order to build trust and respect.

Bonus Tip: Always aim to over-deliver

If you can deliver in seven days but say you'll do it in five, you're bound to disappoint. But if you say you can do it in ten then deliver in seven, your customers will be delighted.

This works with costs too. If you estimate high and it comes in low, your customer will be delighted and the chance of getting repeat business and referrals increases. But if your estimate is too low and you present a bill that is significantly higher than the customer expects, then they are bound to be unhappy – as you would be.

6

HOW TO GENERATE UNLIMITED LEADS FOR YOUR BUSINESS

Do You Know Where Your Customers Come From?

Most people would probably choose advertising as an answer. Or referrals. Or direct mail campaigns. This may seem true, but it's not really accurate.

Your customers come from leads that have been turned into sales. Each customer goes through a two-step process before they arrive ready to spend money on your products or services. They have been converted from a member of a target market, to a lead, and then from a lead, to a customer.

So, would it not stand to reason then, that when you advertise or send any marketing material out to your target market, that you're not really trying to generate customers? Instead, you're trying to generate leads.

When you look at your marketing campaign from this perspective, the idea of generating leads can seem a lot less daunting compared with creating customers. The pressure of closing sales is no longer placed on advertisements or brochures.

From this perspective, the **general purpose of your advertising and marketing efforts is to generate leads from qualified customers.**

Seems easy enough, doesn't it?

Where Are Your Leads Coming From?

If I asked you to tell me the top three ways you generate new sales leads, what would you say?

- Advertising?
- Word of mouth?
- Networking?
- Online?
- Don't know?

The first step toward increasing your leads is in understanding how many leads you currently get on a regular basis, as well as where they come from. Otherwise, how will you know when you're getting more email enquiries, phone calls or walk-in customers?

So, if you don't know where your leads are coming from, start finding out today.

Ask every new customer that contacts you by email, *'How did you find us?'* or *'What brought you to our website today?'*

Ask every new customer that comes through your door, *'How did you hear about us?'* or *'What brought you in store today?'*

Ask every new customer that calls where they found your telephone number. Then, record the information for at least a week.

When you're finished, take a look at your spreadsheet and write your top three lead generators here:

1. _____

2. _____

3. _____

From Lead to Customer: Conversion Rates

Leads mean nothing to your business unless you convert them into customers. You could get hundreds of leads from a single advertisement, but unless those leads result in purchases, it's been a largely unsuccessful (and costly) campaign.

The ratio of leads (potential customers) to transactions (actual customers) is called your conversion rate. Simply divide the number of customers who actually purchased something by the number of customers who inquired about your product or service, and multiply by 100.

$$\frac{\text{No of Transactions}}{\text{No of Leads}} \times 100 = \text{Conversion Rate \%}$$

If, in a given week, you have 879 customers come into your store, and 143 of them purchase something, the formula would look like this:

$$\frac{143 \text{ (Transactions)}}{879 \text{ (Leads)}} \times 100 = 16.27 \% \text{ (Conversion Rate)}$$

What's Your Conversion Rate?

Based on the formula above, you can see that the higher your conversion rate, the more profitable the business.

Your next step is to determine you own current conversion rate. Add up the number of leads you sourced in the last section, and divide that number into the total transactions (sales) that took place in the same week.

Write your conversion rate here: _____%

Quality (or Qualified) Leads

Based on our review of conversion rates, we can see that the number of leads you generate means nothing unless those leads are being converted into customers.

So what affects your ability (and the ability of your team) to turn leads into customers?

- Do you need to improve your scripts?
- Does your product or service need enhancing?
- Do you need to find a more competitive edge in the marketplace?

Maybe.

But the first step toward increasing conversion rates is to evaluate the leads you are currently generating, and make sure those leads are the right ones.

What are Quality Leads?

Potential customers are potential customers, right? Anyone who walks into your store or picks up the phone to call your business could be convinced to purchase from you, right? Not necessarily, but this is a common assumption most business owners make.

Quality leads are the people who are most likely to buy your product or service. They are the qualified buyers who comprise your target market. Anyone might walk in off the street to browse a furniture store – regardless of whether or not they are in the market for a new couch or bed frame. This lead is solely interested in browsing, and is not likely to be converted to a customer.

A quality lead would be someone looking for a new kitchen table, and who specifically drove to the same furniture store because a friend had raved about the service they received that month.

These are the kinds of leads you need to focus on generating.

How Do You Get Quality Leads?

Know your target market

Understand who your ideal customers are – the people who are most likely to buy your product or service. Know their age, sex, income, and purchase motivations. From that information you can determine how best to reach your specific audience.

Focus on the 80/20 rule

A common statistic in business is that 80% of your revenue comes from 20% of your customers. These are your star clients, or your ideal clients. These are the clients you should focus your efforts on recruiting. This is the easiest way to grow your business and your income.

Get specific

Focus not only on who you want to attract, but how you're going to attract them. If you're trying to generate leads from a specific market segment, craft a unique offer to get their attention.

Be proactive

Once you've generated a slew of leads, make sure you have the resources to follow up on them. Be diligent and aggressive, and follow up in a timely manner. You've done to work to get them, now reel them in.

Get More Leads from Your Existing Strategies

Increasing your lead generation doesn't necessarily mean diving in and implementing an expensive array of new marketing strategies. Marketing and customer outreach for the purpose of lead generation can be inexpensive, and bring a high return on investment.

You may already be implementing many of these strategies. With a little tweaking or refinement, you can easily double your leads, and ensure they are more qualified.

Here are some popular ways to generate quality leads:

Direct Mail to Your Ideal Customers

Direct mail is one of the fastest and most effective ways to generate leads that will build your business. It's a simple strategy – in fact, you may already be reaching out to potential clients through direct mail letters with enticing offers.

The secret to doubling your results is to craft your direct mail campaigns specifically for a highly targeted audience of your *ideal* customers.

Your ideal customers are the people who will buy the most of your products or services. They are the customers who will buy from you over and over again, and refer your business to their friends. They are the group of 20% of your clients who make up 80% of your revenue.

Identify your ideal customers

Who are your ideal customers? What is their age, sex, income, location and purchase motivation? Where do they live? How do they spend their money? Be as specific as possible.

Once you have identified who your ideal customers are, you can begin to determine how you can go about reaching them. Will you mail direct to households? Families or retirees? Direct mail lists are available for purchase from a wide range of companies, and can be segregated into a variety of demographic and sociographic categories.

Craft a special offer

Create an offer that's too good to refuse – not for your entire target market, but for your ideal customer. How can you cater to their unique needs and wants? What will be irresistible for them?

For example, if you operate a furniture store, your target market is a broad range of people. However, if you are targeting young families, your offer will be much different from one you may craft for empty-nesters.

Follow-up regularly even after they buy from you

Don't stop at a single mailing. Sometimes people will throw your letter away two or three times before they are motivated to act. Treat your direct mail campaign like a courtship, and understand that it will happen over time.

First send a letter introducing yourself, and your irresistible offer. Then follow up on a monthly basis with additional letters, newsletters, offers, or flyers. Repetition and reinforcement of your presence is how your customer will go from saying, *'Who is this company'* to *'I buy from this company'* and even *'I recommend that you look at how this company can help you.'*

Advertise for Leads

Statistics show that nearly 50% of all purchase decisions are motivated by advertising. It can also be a relatively cost effective way of generating leads.

We've already discussed the importance of ensuring your advertisements are purpose-focused. The general purpose of most advertisements is to increase sales – which starts with leads. However ads that are created solely for lead generation – that is, to get the customers to pick up the phone or walk in the store – are a category of their own.

Lead generation ads are simply designed and create a sense of curiosity or mystery. Often, they feature an almost unbelievable offer. Their purpose is not to convince the customer to buy, but to contact the business for more information.

As always, when you are targeting your ideal audience, you'll need to ensure that your ads are placed prominently in publications that audience reads. This doesn't mean you have to fork out the cash for expensive display ads. Inexpensive advertising in e-mail newsletters, classifieds, and the yellow pages are very effective for lead generation.

Here are some tips for lead generation:

Leverage Low-cost Advertising
If your target audience is technology savvy, consider using Facebook and Google Adwords. Alternatively place ads in the classifieds sections of trade magazines, e-mail newsletters, and online.

Spark Curiosity
Don't give them all the information they need to make a decision. Ask them to contact you for the full story, or the complete details of the seemingly outrageous offer.

Grab them with a Killer Headline
Like all advertising, a compelling headline is essential. Focus on the greatest benefits to the customer, or feature an unbelievable offer.

Referrals Systems & Joint Ventures

A referral system is one of the most profitable systems you can create in your business. The beauty is once it's set up, it often runs itself.

Customers that come to you through referrals are often your 'ideal customers.' They are already trusting and willing to buy. This is one of the most cost-effective methods of generating new business, and is often the most profitable. These referral clients will buy more, faster, and refer further business to your company.

Referrals naturally happen without much effort for reputable businesses, but with a proactive referral strategy you'll certainly double or triple your referrals. Sometimes, you just need to ask!

Here are some easy strategies you can begin to implement today:

Referral Incentives

Give your customers a reason to refer business to you. Reward them with discounts, gifts, or free service in exchange for a successful referral.

Referral Program

Offer new customers a free product or service to get them in the door. Then, at the end of the transaction, give them three more *coupons* for the same free product or service that they can give to their friends. Do the same with their friends. This ongoing program will bring you more business than you can imagine.

Joint Ventures

Forge alliances with non-competitive companies who target your ideal customers. Create cross-promotion and cross-referral direct mail campaigns that benefit both businesses. This is such an important strategy, the whole of Chapter 7 is dedicated to showing you how to set up and profit from joint ventures.

Lead Management Systems

Once your lead generation strategies are in place, you'll also need a system to manage incoming inquiries. You'll need to ensure you receive enough information from each lead to follow up on at a later date.

You'll also need to create a system to organise that information, and track the lead as it is converted into a sale.

Gathering Information from Your Leads

Here is a list of information you should gather from your leads. This list can be customised to the needs of your business, and the type of information you can realistically ask for from your potential customers. Start with the top four and add more information as it becomes available.

- **Company Name**
- **Name of Contact**
- **Email Address**
- **Mobile Phone**
- Alternate Contact Person
- Mailing Address
- Phone Number
- Fax Number
- Website Address
- Product of Interest / Hot buttons

Lead Management Methods

Once you have gathered information from your lead, you'll need a system to organise the information and keep a detailed contact history.

One way to do this is with a database program, but you can also use a variety of hard copy methods.

Electronic Database Programs

- High level of organisation available
- Unlimited space for notes and record-keeping
- Data-entry required
- Simple example: MS Excel
- More sophisticated online tool: Salesforce.com
- Customer Relationship Management Software

Hard copy methods seem be an old fashioned idea, but, like a paper diary or day-planner, they can still work particularly for smaller volumes of customers and for businesses that are not that heavily invested in technology.

Index Cards

- Variety of sizes
- Basic contact information on one side
- Notes on the other side
- Easy to organise and sort

Notebooks

- Best if leads are managed by a single person
- Lots of room for notes
- Inexpensive
- Difficult to re-organise

Business Card Organiser

- Best for small lists – under 100
- Limited space for notes
- No data entry required

For more valuable business & marketing resources please visit

www.MaximumPerformanceAcademy.com

or contact the author directly on

info@ MaximumPerformanceAcademy.com

7

HOW TO PROFIT FROM
JOINT VENTURES

Is this the best kept secret to growing your business?

Did you know that a business just down the street from yours may be able to help double your profits this year? Or does this sound a little too far-fetched?

Maybe. If you operate a retail store that sells car accessories, and the business down the road is a hair salon, you may have a hard time making this happen. However, marketing partnerships between complementary, non-competing businesses can be a financial goldmine when implemented strategically. And your joint venture partner may be just around the corner!

Sometimes referred to as Host Beneficiary Relationships, these partnerships help small and medium-sized businesses tap into very specific target markets and close sales under existing relationships of trust.

Joint venture relationships allow one business (the partner) to add value to their product or service, and another (the beneficiary) to benefit from the impact of a referral. The beauty of this arrangement is that the roles can then be reversed.

Like any marketing strategy, joint ventures don't work for every business all the time. However, they are a great tool to keep in your marketing tool-kit when starting a business, entering new markets, boosting product sales, or any other opportunity that requires a specific and personal approach.

How Can a Joint Venture Help Your Business?

Establishing, planning, and implementing a successful JV campaign is more complex than asking your neighbour to send a letter to his client base with an offer from your company.

As with every other component of your marketing strategy and materials, a JV campaign must be purpose-driven and evaluated to be the best approach to secure your desired results.

However, if your business caters to a broad audience and you have an irresistible offer that is going to have people running through your doors, you may want to consider a simple advertisement that will reach the most people. And if you offer a relatively common product with a low price point, a JV may not be worth the cost and effort involved to set it up.

When will a JV benefit your business?

If you are a Start-up

A company that is just starting out has the most to gain from a JV Relationship. Faced with the standard challenges of establishing a new operation – credibility, product positioning, target market establishment, marketing strategy, etc. – a JV Relationship is an ideal way to get the business off the ground.

Gaining access to a list of potential clients in your target market is an impressive benefit. Getting an established business to communicate your offer on your behalf is an almost guaranteed way to establish your own credibility.

However, start-ups often have the least to offer a *partner* company in exchange for being the *beneficiary*. Trading client lists is not an option in this case. So what's in it for the *partner*?

The partner is seen in the eyes of his customers as providing a reward or an exclusive offer for their continued support and loyalty. The partner business earns goodwill and has an excuse to contact his database for the cost of a simple mailing.

If you are entering a New Market

An established business venturing into new territory is in a prime position to benefit from a JV Relationship. Whether the business is known or unknown in the community, tapping into a refined target list will ensure that the right people are communicated the benefits of the new business' offering.

In exchange, the partner business may benefit from either the beneficiary's client lists in other marketplaces, or the prestige of offering clients an exclusive offer for a new business.

Again, this works best when the target market is highly segmented; otherwise, an advertisement would be a faster and more cost effective strategy.

If you are offering a New Product / Service
As with new marketplaces, launching a new product or service may require tapping into a new or more segmented audience to deliver your message. A JV with the right partner will help to correctly position your offering, and deliver it to an exact audience.

The partner business benefits by offering their loyal clients the first opportunity to purchase or use the products /services of the beneficiary.

Defining Your Target Market

This is crucial in establishing a JV Relationship – just like it is crucial in every other aspect of your marketing plan. Not knowing and understanding your target market will put you on the fast track to business hardship, and waste time and money in the process.

You can determine your target market – or target market segment – based on the purpose or intention for seeking a JV Relationship. Are you reaching out to a new segment of your market? Are you offering a new product or service that may appeal to a specific segment of your market? Are you moving to a new market area and looking to establish yourself amongst your broader target?

Determine your audience and write your target market here – refer back to Chapter 1:

_____

_____

_____

_____

_____

Selecting a Joint Venture Partner

Once you have an idea of who your target market is, you can begin to create a list of potential joint venture partners to approach.

Not every business is going to be interested or willing to engage in this marketing strategy – so doing a little bit of research and positioning your offer is well worth your while. To begin, you will want to draft a long list of all potential partners.

Do this by considering all business types that would be complementary to – but not competing with – your business.

Those businesses that offer a service or product that is connected in some way to your own. For example, if you operate a hair salon, some potential JV partners would include beauty salons, clothing stores, therapists, and perhaps some specialty goods stores.

Or, if you retail car accessories, you might consider a list that includes hardware stores, car washes, car body shops, specialty auto part distributors or mobile car repairs.

Pick up the yellow pages, or conduct an online search for all businesses in your market area that fall under the categories you identified. You may also consider asking your colleagues and associates for ideas and recommendations.

When creating this list, make sure each business falls under these criteria:

Non-competitive
Their offer should be complementary to, but not compete with, your product or service. Make sure you consider this carefully; seemingly non-competitive offers may actually cannibalise your business.

Remember that your customers have a limited amount of money to spend, and if they begin spending money at your partner's business, they might stop spending money at your business.

Same target market

If you and your partner business are not talking to the same customer base, then you're wasting your words on customers who are not likely to buy your service or product. If your partner business has no idea who their target market is, you may also want to consider looking at other partner options.

Start with your customers – your target market or a segment of your target market. What services do they use? What products are they interested in? Thinking about their needs will help you to identify the most effective partner business.

An up-to-date customer contact list

Without this, they aren't worth approaching – but how do you know they have or maintain a customer database? There are a couple of ways.

Pay attention to the type of marketing your potential partner conducts. Do they often send letters to their target market? Direct-mail flyers and other promotional materials? Or do they rely on advertising? Do they send a regular newsletter? They may also hold their customer contact information in their point of sale system – if it is technologically advanced enough to do so.

Positive reputation

As the beneficiary, you need to ensure that the partner who is referring your business to their customers enjoys a good reputation in the community and with its clientele. Otherwise, you are being endorsed by a business that no one respects, which can be damaging for your reputation.

List of Possible JV Partners

Keep track of all potential JV partners using this chart.

Business Name	Contact	Business Type
	Name: Phone: Email:	
	Name: Phone: Email:	
	Name: Phone: Email:	
	Name: Phone: Email:	
	Name: Phone: Email:	
	Name: Phone: Email:	
	Name: Phone: Email:	

Approaching your JV Partners

Once you have created a list of target businesses, it is time to plan your approach. There is some strategy involved in this; you need to convince the partner business to lend their endorsement and customer contact list to you in exchange for something that will benefit them.

Introduce your product or service

Present your offering to the partner business as though you were presenting to your potential customers: heavy on benefits, and light on features. Assume that the partner business has placed themselves in the shoes of their customers, and is evaluating whether your product or service is worthwhile for them.

Provide marketing materials and other supporting information like testimonials and market research to establish your credibility, and your understanding of the people you are trying to reach.

Inform and excite

Provide as much information about how the Joint Venture will work, and be sincere in your efforts. Leave room for their thoughts and contributions to ensure that they buy into the process.

Get them excited about the opportunity you've placed in front of them. Use bright examples, and tell a hypothetical story about one of their customers benefiting from your service. Then, bring it back to the benefits that the relationship or partnership will deliver to their business.

Include an incentive

Be clear about the benefits your JV partner can expect to receive. While you will not always be able to offer something tangible, do your best to offer some incentive to the prospective partner business, or else why would they be interested.

If you are an established business, offer them reverse access to your customer database after the initial mailing. Or, if you have room in your margin, offer them a piece of the profits you receive from their customers. Whatever it is, make sure you articulate how this particular partnership is worth their while.

Communicate your rationale

Tell the partner why you chose to approach them in particular. Do they enjoy a great reputation in the community? Are they a well-known business with a great sense of camaraderie? Compliment them on their business skills and the great relationships they have built with their customers and in the community.

Then, explain how your business can add value to theirs, and allow them to build on the existing relationships with their clients by offering your services.

Reassure

Communicate the benefits of the Joint Venture to the partner, and reassure them that there is no risk involved for them. You are not out to take their profits, or place burden on their resources.

Remind them that you are seeking a complementary business relationship, one that benefits both parties.

Craft Your Message

Once you have secured your partner, put the plan into action as quickly as possible. Offering to write the letter to their customers will not only give you control over the messaging of the offer, but also reduce the time investment required by the partner. The process is simplified for them, and happens sooner for you.

5 Simple Steps to Creating a Joint Venture Relationship

In summary, here are is a five-step roadmap to creating a positive, profit-filled, joint venture:

1. Identify your target market
2. Identify target partner businesses
3. Create a unique offer for each partner business
4. Approach the partner business
5. Draft your letter

Here are some things to think about when you draft your letter;

- Just like sales letters and other marketing collateral, your offer letter should engage the reader and make them feel as though their needs and interests are cared for.

- The letter should position the partner as a thoughtful service provider who sought out an offer specifically for the target audience.

- Your offer should be strong and slightly outrageous. Give deep discounts, or free services, exclusively to this target audience.

- Remember to acknowledge the needs and troubles of your reader, and position your product or service as the answer or solution.

- Include an incentive to act quickly. Ensure your offer is time-sensitive or of limited quantity, but do so credibly.

Points to Remember

Make mistakes in small batches

If you are unsure about the accuracy of your target market – do a test run. Send a small batch of 50-100 letters to a small group of people, and measure the response.

Alternately, you can send three different letters to each third of your target market, and evaluate which offer is acted on the most. This is of benefit for both the partner and the beneficiary business because the response rate of the target market is tested, as are their purchase motivations.

Create benefits for the partner business

Remember that there must be an incentive for the partner business, or the partnership is not worth the time investment. It is important to consider this, and plan ahead before you approach the partner business. Create a number of options for the partner to choose from, whether it is using your database after the initial mailing, or sharing a piece of the profits.

Be honest

If you are working with several businesses in your area on different offers, make sure each business knows and is comfortable with the arrangement. Ensure that each offer is distinctive and each partner is benefiting from the arrangement without competing with other partner businesses. This is just good business sense.

Rest on the strength of your offer

With a strong offer, your JV campaign will be on the path to success. Make it something your audience can't refuse. Your offer should not only be enticing and engaging for your audience, but should also benefit the partner in reputation. Their customers should feel valued and appreciative toward the partner for bringing your offer forward.

Repeat

Once you've established one successful JV partnership, keep going! This technique is a valuable way to promote your business and your unique products and services, and can be repeated several times each year with several different partner businesses.

Joint Venture Letter Template – to amend as appropriate

[Headline in bold at the top of the page – strong statement or question]

[Optional sub-headline to explain or answer the question/statement]

Dear [name],

I am writing to you as one of our existing customers because I have discovered an exciting new [product or service] that will [describe how it will meet a need or solve a problem].

[Beneficiary business name] is a [describe business type] that [describe business function]. I recently met with the owner, and was able to secure an unbelievable rate for you as one of my existing customers. The [product or service] is [describe product or service briefly].

Customers who have already purchased have said:

- *[list testimonials in bullet form]*

[Describe limited time or quantity], we are pleased to offer you [describe unique offer here]. This is an opportunity you will not find anywhere else, and an offer that will not be available in stores.

I hope you will be able to take advantage of this amazing [product or service].

Sincerely, [your name & contact details]

Joint Venture Worksheet

Target Market:

Potential Partner 1: Name: Business Type:	**Unique Offer:**
Partner Benefits:	**Date Contacted:**
	☐ Accepted ☐ Follow-up
Notes:	

Target Market:

Potential Partner 2: Name: Business Type:	**Unique Offer:**
Partner Benefits:	**Date Contacted:**
	☐ Accepted ☐ Follow-up
Notes:	

Why I like Joint Ventures

So what do you think? Are joint ventures the best kept secret to growing *your* business?

The reason I like joint ventures and recommend them whenever I can to my clients is that, in a world dominated by big brands and massive corporate giants, joint ventures provide a genuine opportunity for smaller businesses to punch above their weight and quickly increase brand awareness, gain new customers and market share. And if three businesses can get together and promote each other's products and services the effects can be exponential for them all.

Here is a letter template and worksheet to get you on your way with your first joint venture.

Good luck!

For more valuable business & marketing resources please visit

www.MaximumPerformanceAcademy.com

or contact the author directly on

info@ MaximumPerformanceAcademy.com

8

HOW TO USE PRESS RELEASES FOR INSTANT PROFIT

Make Your Business News

The best kind of free advertising is an article in the newspaper, or a story on the radio, shining positive light on your business. Although not strictly speaking advertising, just like a testimonial, the printed words of a journalist are up to ten times more valuable than the words in your own advertising. Likewise, negative articles and reviews can cause just as much impact on your business – the kind of impact you don't want.

So how do you get your business news into the press? Better still, how do you make sure the press gets positive, accurate information about your business?

The simplest way to communicate with the media is through press releases. Press releases are a standard form of communication with the media, used to announce, communicate, and correct *newsworthy* information.

Press releases are not sales letters, or even newsletters. Their purpose is not to make a sale – although they may lead to sales – because they are not written for your customer. Their purpose is to communicate news to the people that write the news, in a way that makes them take notice and care about what you have to say.

What are Effective Press Releases?

Effective press releases get your story covered. They hook editors on your angle, and encourage journalists to write about your news. They are concise, engaging, and written *with the media in mind*. If your business is looking for local coverage, choose a local paper or radio station; if you have technical product, find the appropriate trade journal.

It's a good idea to sit down with your colleagues, family, and friends to test your story idea for newsworthiness. They'll be able to help you brainstorm angles and strategically plan your release.

Before you sit down to write your press release, ask yourself the following questions:

Is your story newsworthy?

If you're not used to writing press releases, spend some time thinking about this question. Of course your story is newsworthy to *you*, but why should other people care? Why does this story *matter* to the newspaper's readers? Newsworthy items are relevant, current, useful, and of importance to the community.

They provide answers to the five *W's* (who, what, where, when and why).

Do you have an angle?

So your item is newsy, but what's the *angle*? Sure your company has had a record year for revenue, but what makes it unique? What makes your news an engaging story that is relevant to people outside your office? A press release should have at least one solid angle, or story idea, for the journalist. If the media have to spend time finding the story buried in your press release, you have an unlikely chance of getting covered.

Is now the right time to tell your story?

You may have a newsy story and an interesting angle, but is now the best time to tell your story? Be strategic about timing – for the benefit of your business, and for the likelihood of getting coverage. If you're a retailer featuring a new product line in October, is there benefit in waiting until November to announce your news, when customers are shopping for the Christmas? Did the newspaper you're targeting just run a big feature on the competition? Are you waiting on other potential news that you could announce at the same time?

Is your story true?

Reporting inaccurate or exaggerated facts is bad form, and can wreak havoc on your reputation. While you wouldn't do this intentionally, check to make sure you're not embellishing the facts to create a more interesting story. Journalists are trained to spot when something doesn't look right.

Who needs to know your story?

When you craft a press release, you need to be clear on who you want to read your story. Once you know exactly who your target audience is, you can narrow your focus down to the media that reach that audience. From there, you can cater your press release to the journalists who work for those outlets.

Writing Effective Press Releases

Here are some general rules and guidelines for crafting the perfect press release. Be prepared to write a few different versions, and make substantial edits; it takes a while to get it right. If writing is not your strongest skill, consider hiring a freelance writer to describe your news. Some online press release distribution services also offer writing services, so consider your options.

Craft an attention grabbing headline

Just like advertisements, you have seconds to grab the media's attention with your headline. The headline should tell the story and answer the question *why does it matter?* Or, *why should I care?* Keep in mind that the headline you start with may need revising when you've finished the article.

Spend time on the introductory paragraph

The introductory paragraph is the post important part of the press release. It answers the five *W's* and provides enough detail to make the journalist or editor read on. Write a few different introductions, each with a different story angle, and see which one has the most impact. If the introduction doesn't hook your reader, consider your press release in the recycle bin.

Write for the newspaper

Make your release easy to read, and easy for the journalist to work with. Occasionally, especially in communities with limited reporting resources, press releases are run with only some slight rewriting. In the best case, your release becomes the base for a feature article. Spend some time reading the publication you're targeting, and notice the style in which it is written.

Notice newspaper style

Generally, articles (and press releases) are written in an inverse pyramid format, where the most important information is as the top, and less important information follows in decreasing order of importance.

Use simple language

Sentences written in simple style, with minimal description, and without unnecessary embellishments, are all that should appear in the release. Make sure each word has a purpose, and keep it tight. Only use the space you need to tell the story, no more.

Use examples to support your facts

If you're sending a press release highlighting an achievement or accomplishment, prove it. Show the media that there are events and facts to back up your claims – cause and effect. This illustrates and tells a story, which is always more interesting and engaging than proud statements and quotes.

Skip industry jargon

While industry phrases and terms may mean something to your colleagues and clients, they mean nothing to the media and the general public. Limit the amount of jargon you include in your release, and provide succinct explanations for uncommon terms you must use. Keep the language simple and easy to understand.

Use quotes sparingly

Quotes are great ways to back up facts, add personality to your news, and include a new voice in the release. When writing quotes, ensure that the person being quoted is named before their quote, and that they are relevant and important to the story.

Keep the quotes authentic, concise, and limited to two sources. Quotes from more than two sources in one release can become cluttered and confusing.

Tell them who you are

At the end of the release, be sure to include a short paragraph about your company that describes who you are, what you do, and a brief history.

Include as much contact information as possible

Include one or two contact names, their titles, phone numbers, email addresses, website address and cell phone numbers (if necessary). Make it as easy as possible for media to contact you.

Include a photograph & a caption

Increase your chances of getting published and getting noticed by including an eye-catching photograph with your press release. And to make it as easy as possible for the journalist, write a caption to go with it that explains who is in the photograph and why it is important to the story.

Distribution

Media Target List

A database of local of media is a key tool for any small business. Whether this list is used for an advertising campaign, or media relations, it is important to know the players in your local media market.

Depending on your needs – and the size of your desired reach – there are a number of ways to create this list. If you are sticking to local and regional daily media, you can easily create and maintain your database in house.

If you're looking to have a broader reach, there are a number of online services that provide access to customer media lists on a one-time or subscriber basis. These services typically have the most up to date information, as well as more detailed information about media contacts that you would not find on the internet.

This list should include the name of the publication, the type of publication, the publication's frequency, a contact name, phone number and email address. In most outlets, journalists are assigned to *beats* or subjects to cover, like business, crime, health, and community. If you know that you are targeting the business section of the newspaper, make sure your release ends up in the hands of the business editor or reporter. Just like your marketing materials, you need to make sure your message ends up in the right hands.

Email Distribution

The easiest and most common form of press release distribution is by email. However, journalists are bombarded by emails and it is easy for yours to get lost in the pile. Here are some tips to make sure it gets read, and not immediately deleted.

Don't send attachments

Put your news release in text format in the body of the email with simple formatting to make sure it gets read. Attachments get stuck in junk mail filters, and emails from unknown sources with attachments get deleted.

Put the headline in the subject line

Make sure you grab the attention of your recipient with the subject line to entice them to open the email. Don't assume that everything you send will be opened. Generic subject lines get buried in inboxes, or deleted.

Include a personal introduction or pitch

While this can be time consuming, this is a nice strategy to implement when sending your release to your top ten media targets. Write a personal greeting before the release that hooks them on the story angle immediately. Keep it short, and if possible, include an acknowledgement of one of their recent stories that relates to your news.

Over time, getting to know your local journalists can pay off. You can become the industry expert they contact for comments when they are running relevant stories and need someone to provide a quote.

Distribution Services

There are also a number of reputable press release distribution networks that will distribute your release to a broad audience. Sites like prnewswire.com allow you to send your release to a specific market. These services also often provide writing or editing assistance, and can be valuable one-stop-shops.

Top 10 Press Release Mistakes

1. Errors in Grammar

Journalists are professional writers with a solid understanding of grammar and punctuation. Don't distract them from your news with spelling mistakes and poorly composed sentences. If writing isn't your strong suit, hire someone to write or proofread your release before you send it.

2. Too much content

The press release is intended to hook the editor, communicate the facts, and make sure it is newsworthy. Once the editor or journalist is pursuing your story, you can provide them with more information and people to talk to. Stick to two pages double-spaced, max.

3. Too little content

You want to keep your release short and simple, but make sure you include all the necessary facts to support and illustrate the story. Make sure the five *W's* are answered, and all the correct contact information has been provided.

4. Not blind-copying recipients

Before you send your release, double check that you haven't put all recipients in the *To* field of your email. Doing so announces who you're sending the information to, when all the recipients are competitors looking to run the story first. Use the BCC field and then address the release to yourself.

5. Sending first thing Monday morning

A journalist's inbox is the most overloaded first thing in the morning – especially on Mondays. Typically, journalists will meet with editors in the morning to review editorial assignments, then work to a mid-afternoon deadline. The best time to call and email a reporter is mid-to-late afternoon, when their deadline has passed and their inbox has been sorted through.

6. Releases that read like ads

Your press release is not an advertisement, so don't write it like one. A journalist's job is to communicate pertinent, relevant, newsworthy information to their audience, not convince them to buy your product. Avoid overused advertising catch phrases like *limited time offer,* and *this won't last long!* Your job here is to communicate, not to sell.

7. Not securing permission

Make sure you have permission to mention companies other than yours, to quote sources, and to submit images of your clients and employees to the press. Not having permission for these items can result in your story getting pulled at the last minute.

8. Sending to multiple editors at one outlet

Pick the editor who will be most interested in your news at each target news organisation, and send your release to them only. This will avoid duplication of efforts at the outlet. Often, if an editor is not interested in your news, but knows an associate editor who will be, they will give you another contact name or pass the news on directly.

9. Not being relevant for the media targeted

The local motorbike magazine doesn't care about news from a baby clothing business. Make sure the media on your list are the media who would realistically cover your news. Sending information that does not align with the publication's subject matter will show you haven't done your research.

10. Following up the day you send the release

It may take a few days for an editor to respond to – or even read – your release. Be patient, and wait at least a week before following up. Even then, don't assume that your release has been read or remembered. Use the opportunity to pitch the editor over the phone on your story idea, or try a new angle.

Use the following press release template and examples to write your own press releases and increase the profile of your business.

The Media Contacts form at the end of this chapter is for you to keep a record of any contacts from local newspapers, radio stations and other media outlets as well as freelance journalists who you may want to write for you.

Press Release Template

For Immediate Release: Date

SMART, CATCHY HEADLINE IN BOLD, CAPITALS, CENTERED AT THE TOP OF THE PAGE

Sub-headline, If Some Description is Required, In Title Case Beneath Headline

This is the Introduction. This paragraph, which should not be indented, should include the pertinent information – *who, what, where, and why it matters to the editor's audience.* Put yourself in the editor or journalist's shoes – why should they cover this story? Why does it matter to their readers? Is it newsworthy?

The second paragraph should elaborate on the content from the lead paragraph, and usually includes a quote from a key person (Managing Director, CEO, etc.) that communicates a feeling, belief, or general view of the issue.

The third paragraph is a brief history of the event, achievement or subject of the news release. How did the company get there? What did they do to achieve this? How long have they been working to get here?

The fourth paragraph can be another quote – share another perspective or a rationale behind any controversial issues. It can also elaborate or continue from the first quote.

The fifth paragraph is about the audience – how will they benefit? What does this mean to them? What are the next steps? *The audience can include a residential community, business community, industry, etc.*

The sixth paragraph can highlight key points in bullet format – deadlines, dates, milestones, report highlights, key features, event details, etc.

The last paragraphs are used to explain more about the company – what have they done that is related to this or newsworthy? Explain more about the process – how do you achieve this? Include any other pertinent information that the audience will need to know about next steps, what to watch for etc. Include more quotes from key sources.

High resolution images of (xxx) are available upon request

END *This shows to the reader that the news release is over.*

Media Contact *no more than two contacts, these people must be available as soon as the release is sent out*

Name
Position
Organisation
Contact details (Phone / Email)

Press Release Example: New Product

For Immediate Release: Date

MUMS ON WHEELS TO DELIVER NUTRITIOUS MEALS AT SCHOOL THIS SEPTEMBER

New Lunchtime Service to Provide Kids with Balanced Snacks and Meals

Attention busy mums: take lunches off your to-do list. Mums on Wheels is expanding this September, providing daily lunch service for primary school pupils with busy families. Parents can now subscribe to daily or weekly deliveries, and trust that convenient, healthy bag lunches are arriving at their children's classroom.

Barbara Jones, Mums on Wheels co-founder and dietician says '*As a mother, one of my biggest challenges is making sure my two sons go to school with a healthy and balanced lunch. Between grocery shopping, preparing meals, packing lunch, and making sure it winds up in their backpacks, it was taking up a lot of my time.*' Mums on Wheels prepares lunches fresh every morning, then delivers to 20 primary schools by 12:30pm. Lunch menus vary from wraps and sandwiches, to cheese and crackers, with an assortment of seasonal vegetables, fruit and a cookie.

Mums on Wheels offers daily and weekly meal options, and caters to dietary and allergy requirements. Starting at just £3 a day, the service is affordable for every family and can be customised to a specific budget. Family rates are also available for parents with multiple children in school.

The innovative service is the brainchild of Barbara Jones and Lindsay Lee who established the meal service last year to deliver lunches once a week to local primary schools. Jones and Lee plan to expand the service to hot items next year, when they move to an expanded kitchen facility.

To register, contact Mums on Wheels at (telephone number) or www.healthylunchesforkids.co.uk. All primary students will be bringing home an information form during the first week of school this year.

END

Media Contact   Barbara Jones, Co-Founder
Mums on Wheels
Contact details

Press Release Example: Accomplishment

For Immediate Release: Date

CARR'S CARPET CLEANING SWEEPS UP WITH BUSINESS OF THE YEAR AWARD

Local Business Wins Four Accolades at Annual Chamber of Commerce Event

You could say that Carr's Carpet Cleaning Services truly *cleaned up* this year; the local business was honoured with an award in four categories at the annual Chamber of Commerce Business Awards. Carr's Carpet Cleaning earned Employer of the Year Award, Story of the Year Award, Fastest Growing Business, and the prestigious Business of the Year Award.

Jerry Owens, the owner of Carr's Carpet Cleaning said today *'We are thrilled and amazed at the generous recognition we received as a company last night. These awards were earned by every member of our staff, and the terrific job they do servicing our clients.'*

Carr's Carpet Cleaning was established by local resident Jerry Owens just three years ago at the age of 22. Starting out with a small business loan from his grandfather, Gerald Carr, Owens has built the company into a thriving business of 25 employees, serving five communities in the region. This year, Owens introduced three new services: furniture cleaning, duct cleaning, and stain protection treatment.

Peter Smith, President of the Chamber of Commerce described the difficulties of picking the award category *winners 'It is always such a challenge to decide on a single recipient in each of the award categories, especially since there are so many reputable businesses in our community that deserve recognition. However, we were very impressed with Mr. Owen's story, and the incredible growth of Carr's Carpet Cleaning over the last year.'*

Carr's Carpet Cleaning provides regular cleaning services to customers across the region, and offers free custom quotations, and a full satisfaction, money-back guarantee. Carr's uses a premium steam method for stain removal that eliminates marks and odours in a single treatment. With two brand new cleaning units, Carr's also now offers complete stain prevention treatments – an ideal worry-free service for families with young children.

The Chamber of Commerce Business Awards are held annually to recognise business achievement in the area. For a complete list of award recipients, please contact the Chamber directly at (telephone number). Deadline for nominations for next year's awards is 31 August.

High resolution images of the awards presentations are available upon request

END

Media Contacts

Jerry Owens, Owner	Peter Smith, President
Carr's Carpet Cleaning	Chamber of Commerce
Contact details	Contact details

Press Release Example: Controversy

***Note:** When faced with a controversy that may affect the reputation of your business, consider hiring a professional public relations firm. These professionals are trained to handle challenging media relations scenarios, and can help to determine the best strategy for information disclosure.*

For Immediate Release: Date

HOLIDAY SPRUCE OFFERS FREE CHRISTMAS TREE REPLACEMENT TO ALL RESIDENTS
Trees Sprayed with Dangerous Chemical to be Removed and Replaced at No Charge

Holiday Spruce announced today that 75 per cent of the Christmas Trees for sale at their farm have been mistreated with a chemical component that may be dangerous if repeatedly inhaled or accidentally ingested. The Christmas tree farm is offering free removal and replacements for all families affected.

Holiday Spruce Manager Tim Smith has responded quickly. *'We at Holiday Spruce are appalled by the circumstances that allowed our customers and families to take home mistreated Christmas trees. We sincerely apologise to the families affected by these events, and are committed to removing and replacing every single tree within the next four days.'*

Holiday Spruce is currently investigating the cause of the chemical mistreatment, and has closed their farm for the season.

All customers who have purchased their holiday trees from the firm are asked to contact their replacement line at (telephone number).

'We have maintained a record of each purchase made this year, and are currently in the process of contacting customers and arranging for immediate removal,' says Smith. *'Holiday Spruce will be purchasing trees from alternative suppliers, and delivering them to clients within the next four days.'*

Holiday Spruce is a seasonal tree farm that has been in operation for nearly 15 years. A family favourite for Christmas tree purchases, the farm also offers school group tours with hot dogs, and roasted chestnuts.

END

Media Contact   Tim Smith, Manager
                           Holiday Spruce
                           Contact details

Media Contacts

Outlet	Type	Name	Email / Phone

9

HOW TO CREATE REPEAT BUSINESS & HAVE CLIENTS THAT PAY, STAY & REFER

Great Customer Service is the Ultimate Secret to Success

When it comes to marketing and generating more income, most business owners are focused outward.

They've carefully established and segmented their target market, and created specific offers and messages for each market segment. They spend thousands in advertising and direct mail campaigns in hot pursuit of more leads, more customers, and more foot traffic.

While this is an effective way to build a business, it is costly and time consuming. It requires constant and consistent effort, and while this approach does generate results, those results quickly disappear when the effort stops or becomes less intense.

Successful businesses that see sustained growth have a double-edged marketing strategy. They focus their efforts *outward* – on new potential customers and marketing – as well as *inward* – on existing customers and referral business.

These successful businesses have leveraged their existing efforts to generate more revenue. Simply put, their customers buy from them over and over again.

For most businesses, this is the easiest way to increase their revenues. Simple customer loyalty strategies and outstanding customer service are often all you need to dramatically increase your sales – from the customers you already have.

The Cost of Your Customers

Do you know how much it costs your business to buy a new customer?

Each new customer that walks through your door – with the exception of referrals – has cost you money to acquire. You have spent money on advertising and promotions to generate leads and turn those leads into customers.

For example, if you have placed an advertisement in your local newspaper for £1,000, and the advertisement brings in 10 customers, you have paid £100 to acquire each customer. You would need to ensure each of those customers spent at least £200 to cover your margin and break even.

Alternately, if you spent two hours of your time and £10 per month on an email marketing program to send a newsletter to your existing database of customers, and you bring in 10 customers as a result – each customer has cost you £1.

Generating more repeat business means focusing on the marketing strategies that aim to keep your existing customers instead of purchasing new ones – effectively reducing the cost of attracting new customers to your business.

These strategies are simple to implement, and don't require much time investment. Just a solid understanding of how to make customers want to come back and spend more of their money

Keeping Your Customers

Marketing strategies that focus on keeping your current customer base are easy and enjoyable to implement. They allow you to build real relationships with the people you do business with, instead of dealing with a revolving door of people on the other end of your sales process.

Repeat customers create a community of people around your business that presumably share the same needs, desires and frustrations. The information you gain from these customers (market research) can help you strengthen your understanding of your target audience, and more accurately segment it.

Remember – 80% of your revenue comes from 20% of your customers. Always focus on these customers. They are ideal customers that you want to recruit, and hold on to.

Customer Service: Make them love buying from you

Every business – even those with excellent service standards can improve the service they provide their customers. Customer service seems to be a dying concept in most businesses; more focus seems to be placed on the speed of the transaction. These days you can even go to the grocery store now and not speak to a single sales associate thanks to self-serve checkouts.

To improve your company's customer service standards, take a survey of your customers and your employees to brainstorm ways you can improve the experience of buying from your business.

Successful customer service standards – those that make your customers *buy* – are:

Consistent

The standards are up kept by every person in your organisation. Expectations are clear and followed through. Customers know what to expect, and choose your business because of those expectations.

Convenient

It is nearly effortless for the customer to spend money at your place of business. Convenience can take many forms – location, product selection, value-added services like delivery – and it is also consistent.

Customer-driven

The service the customer receives is exactly how they would like to be treated when buying your product or service. It is reflective of your target market, and appropriate to their lifestyle. Customers would probably not appreciate white linen tablecloths at a fast food restaurant, but they would appreciate a *service in 2-minutes or less* guarantee.

Keep in touch with Newsletters

A regular newsletter is an easy, time-effective, and inexpensive marketing strategy to implement. Unfortunately, many small businesses think these are too time consuming and too expensive to adopt as part of their marketing strategy.

The most popular type of newsletter distribution is email. This will cost your business as little at £10 per month for an email marketing service subscription, and can be customised to your business. However, email is not the only way to deliver a newsletter.

Here is an easy five-step process to starting a company newsletter:

Step 1. Pick your audience

- New customers?
- Market segment?
- Existing customers?

Step 2. Choose what you're going to say

- Company news?
- Feature product?
- New offer?

Step 3. Determine how you're going to say it

- Articles?
- Bullet points?
- Pictures?

Step 4. Decide how it's going to get to your audience

- Email?
- Mail?
- In-store?

Step 5. Track your results

- How many people opened it?
- Read it?
- Took action?

Value Added Service: Surprise your customers!

Adding value to your business is an effective way of getting your customers back. Every person I know would choose a mattress store that offered free delivery over one that did not, it's that simple.

However a word of warning, don't offer your customers something free if it is not something that they value. Most consumers would value free shipping or delivery, but this may not be important in a B2B transaction. Giving away free shipping in that situation could end up costing you a lot of money and adding little or no perceived value to your customers.

Here are some ways that you can add value to your business:

Feature your expertise

Use your knowledge to provide additional value to your customers. Offer a free consumer guide with every enquiry or a special report with every purchase.

Add convenience services

Offer a service that makes their purchase easier, or more convenient. The best example of this is offering free shipping or delivery for consumers, although this may not be of value to a B2B customer.

Offer new products or services

Feature top of the line or exclusive products, available only at your business. Offer a new service or profile a new staff member with niche expertise.

Package complementary services

Packaging like items together creates an increase in perceived value. This is great for start-up kits.

Value added services generate repeat customers in one of two ways:

First, impress them on their first visit

Impress you customer with great service, a product that meets their needs, and then wow them with something extra that they weren't expecting. Get them to associate the experience of dealing with your business with happy surprises, and create a perception of higher value.

Then, entice them to come back

The introduction of a new value-added service can be enough to convince a customer to buy from you again. Their initial purchase established a trust and knowledge of your business and its processes. They will want to be included in anything new you have to offer – especially if there is exclusivity. It is easier to attract clients that have purchased from you than potential clients who have not.

You can also use value added services to drive referrals, which are the cheapest and best source of new customers.

Customer Loyalty Programmes

Another simple way to keep in touch with existing customers and keep them coming back to you is to create a customer loyalty programme.

These programmes do not have to be complicated or costly, and are relatively easy to maintain once they have been implemented. These programmes also help you gain more information on your customers and their purchasing habits. But don't start one if you can't keep it going – loyalty programmes can bring in quick benefits, but are really a longer term strategy.

Here are some examples of simple loyalty programmes that you can implement:

Free product or service

Give your customers every 10th (or 6th) product or service free. Produce stamp cards with your logo and contact information on it. A neat little trick here is to *pre-stamp* the first few spaces as it increases the perceived value and generates more repeat customers. Works well for coffee and car washes – how can you adapt it for your business?

Reward discount vouchers

Give your customers a certain percentage of their purchase back in vouchers that can only be spent in-store. Produce *funny money* with your logo and brand.

Rewards points

Give your customers a certain number of points for every pound they spend. These points can be spent in-store, or on special items you bring in which can only be obtained by redeeming points.

Membership benefits

Give members access to VIP benefits that are not available to other customers. Produce membership cards or give out membership numbers.

Remember that in order for this strategy to work, you and your team have to understand and promote it. The programme itself becomes a product that you sell.

For more valuable business & marketing resources please visit

www.MaximumPerformanceAcademy.com

or contact the author directly on

info@ MaximumPerformanceAcademy.com

10

HOW TO PROFIT FROM INTERNET MARKETING

There is more to the Internet than Online Shopping

The internet is today's primary consumer research tool. If your business does not have a credible online presence, it is harder for customers to find and choose your business over the competition. With virtually the whole world online, it is no wonder that individuals and businesses in all industries are looking to the internet to enhance their marketing strategies.

Luckily, it has never been easier to establish and maintain a comprehensive online presence. Internet marketing, also referred to as online marketing, online advertising or e-marketing, is the fastest growing medium for marketing.

But it is not just company websites that users are viewing. Blogs, consumer reviews, chat rooms and a variety of social media are growing rapidly in popularity.

The internet is a very powerful tool for businesses if used strategically and effectively. It can be a cost saving alternative to traditional marketing approaches, and may be the most effective way to communicate with your target customer.

A major advantage of the internet is that you are always open. Users can access your business 24 hours a day, 7 days a week, and depending on your business and the purpose of the website, visitors can also purchase goods at any time.

Internet Marketing for Everyone

The internet is a great way to create product and brand awareness, develop relationships with customers and share and exchange information. You can't afford not be taking advantage of online marketing opportunities because your competition is probably already there.

Internet marketing can take on many different forms. By creating maintaining a website for your business, you are reaching out to a new customer base. You can have full control over the messages that users are receiving and have a global reach, if that is what you want.

Internet marketing can be very cost effective. If you have a strong email database of your customers, an e-newsletter will be cheaper and more effective than post mail. You can deliver time sensitive materials immediately and can update your subscribers instantaneously.

An increasing number of customers are first researching products, services and companies online, whether it be to compare products, complete a sale, or look for a future employer. Most people in the 18-35 age group obtain all of their information online—including news, weather and product research.

Internet Marketing Strategies

Internet marketing – like all other elements of your marketing campaign – needs to have clear goals and objectives. Creating brand and product awareness will not happen overnight so it is important to budget accordingly, ensuring there is money set aside for maintenance of the website and analytics.

Be flexible with ideas and options—do your research first, try out different options, then test and measure the results. Metrics and evaluations can be updated almost immediately and should be monitored regularly. By keeping an eye out for what online marketing strategies are working and which are not, it will be easier to create a balanced portfolio of marketing techniques. You might find that in certain geographical areas, certain marketing strategies are more effective than others.

This list is by no means the full extent of options available for marketing online, but it is a good place to start when deciding which options are best suited to your company.

Create a Website

The primary use for the internet is information seeking, so you should provide your customers with information about your company first hand. You have more control over your branding and messaging and can also collect visitor information to determine what types of internet users are accessing your website.

Build an email list of Visitors

This is probably the most important purpose of a commercial website; to gather email addresses of visitors so that you can keep in touch with them by email, continuously educate them about the benefits of using your offerings and the risks of going elsewhere until they are ready to commit to purchase.

You've already seen in an earlier chapter how email marketing works so we don't need to go through that again here. Just remember that, in order to harvest email addresses from your website visitors you need a call to action that makes them an offer they can't refuse; an *Exclusive Report, An Insider's View of the Market, Seven Secrets that other providers won't tell you*, something that grabs the attention and makes them respond.

This strategy may not be appropriate for the larger corporate website, or for when you login to do your online banking, but these websites fulfil a different purpose. If the purpose of your website is to increase sales then building an email list of visitors should be top of the list of what you want it to achieve.

Social Media

Social media can be a blessing and a curse. Yes it gives you the opportunity to interact instantly with your customers and prospects but it can also be a huge distraction and a waste of valuable resources. As with all marketing, Social Media requires an implementation strategy. If you are selling B2B you may want to focus your efforts on LinkedIn. Facebook and Twitter may be more appropriate for B2C sales. One method of using Social Media is to drive visitors to your website, from where you can harvest their email address and enrol then into your email marketing program.

Search Engine Optimisation

Since search engines comprise over 50% of the most visited sites globally, you can go through your website to make it more search engine friendly with the aim to increase your organic search listing. An organic search listing refers to listings in search engine results that appear in order of relevance to the entered search terms.

You may wish to repeat key words multiple times throughout your website and write the copy on your site not only with the end reader in mind, but also search engines.

Remember when you design your website that any text that appears in Flash format is not recognised by search engines. If your entire website is built on a Flash platform, then you will have a poor organic search listing.

Pay Per Click Advertising

If you find that visitors access your website after searching for it first on a search engine, then it may be beneficial to advertise on those websites and bid on keywords associated with your company.

These advertisements will appear at the top of the page or along the left side of the search results on a search engine. You can have control over the specific geographic area you wish to target, set a monthly budget and have the option of being charged only when a user clicks on your link.

Online Directories

Listing your business in an online directory can be an inexpensive and effective online marketing strategy.

However, you need to be able to distinguish your company from the plethora of competitors that may exist. Likely, you will need to complement this strategy with other brand awareness campaigns.

Banner Advertising

These advertisements can have positive or negative effects based on the reputation and customer perception of the website on which you are advertising. These advertisements should be treated in the same way as print advertisements you might place in local newspapers or other publications.

Online Videos

With the growing popularity of sites such as You Tube, it is evident that people love researching online and being able to find video clips of the information they are seeking. Depending on your small business, you may want to upload informational videos or tutorials about your products or services.

Although it may seem daunting, online videos are surprisingly easy and enjoyable to create. With a little planning and a small investment in equipment, you could have a video online in considerably less time than it takes to produce a newsletter, brochure on other comparable marketing material.

Blogging

Blogging can be a fun and interactive way to communicate with users. A blog is traditionally a website maintained by an individual user that has regular entries, similar to a diary. These entries can be commentary, descriptions of events, pictures, videos, and more. Companies can use blogging as a way to keep users updated on current information and allow them to post comments on your blog. If blogging is something you wish to invest in, make sure that it is regularly updated and monitored.

Top 10 Mistakes to Avoid

1. Failure to measure ROI

Which metrics are you using? Are your visitors actually motivated to purchase or sign up? If the benefits of your online campaign are not greater than the costs incurred, then you may wish to re-evaluate your strategy.

2. Poor Web Design

This can leave a poor impression of your company on the visitor. A poor design could frustrate visitors if they are not able to easily find what they went on your site to look for and also does not build trust. If customers do not trust your company or your website, you will not be able to complete the sale and develop a longer relationship with that customer. You also need to include privacy protection and security when building trust.

This also includes ensuring all information on the website is current and having customer service available if users are experiencing difficulty or cannot find the information they are seeking. This could be as simple as providing a Contact Us email or telephone number for support.

3. Becoming locked into an advertising strategy early

Remember that successful companies generally use a variety of marketing methods when creating a marketing strategy so avoid putting all of your eggs in one basket. Online marketing is a very valuable tool, but depending on your business and your target markets, other marketing approaches may be better options for you. If this is your first time making a significant investment into online marketing, you may want to remain flexible and adapt your strategy based on feedback received and by researching and analysing different options.

4. Acting without researching

Similar to becoming locked into an advertising strategy early, this mistake implies not dutifully testing and researching different online marketing options. For example, if your target customer is aged 65+ and you are spending all of your marketing efforts into creating a blogging website (where the average ages of bloggers are 18-35), then you are likely not going to have a successful campaign. This sounds obvious, but there are plenty of businesses that find out the hard way when they see in retrospect what should have been obvious.

5. Assuming more visitors means more sales

You have to go back to your original goals and the purpose of your company. More visitors may not mean more sales if your website is used primarily for information and customers purchase their products elsewhere. The opposite could also be true. You could have an increase in sales without an increase in unique visitors if your current customer base is very loyal and willing to spend lots of money.

Often people will collect information online about products they wish to purchase because it is easier to compare options, but they purchase in person. Even though shopping online is becoming quite popular, people still prefer to see and feel the physical product before purchasing.

6. Failing to follow up with customers that purchase

This is one of the most important aspects of running a business. Return sales can account for between 60% and 90% of total revenue. It's no wonder that organisations are always trying to maintain loyal customers and may have customer relationship management systems in place. It is easier to get a happy customer to purchase again than it is to get a new customer to purchase for the first time.

7. Not incorporating online marketing into the business plan

By ensuring that your online marketing plan is fully integrated and accurately represents your organisation's overall goals and objectives, the business plan will be more comprehensive and encompassing.

8. Trying to discover your own best practices

It is very beneficial to use trial and error to determine the best online strategy from your company, but do not be afraid to do your research and learn from what other have already figured out. There will be many cases where someone was in a very similar position as you and they may have some suggestions and secrets that they wish to share. Researching in advance can save a great deal of time and money.

9. Spending too much too fast

Although it may be cheaper than traditional marketing approaches, internet marketing does have its costs. You have to consider the software and hardware designs, maintenance, distribution, supply chain management, and the time that will be required. You don't want to spend your entire marketing budget all at once.

10. Getting distracted by metrics that are not relevant

As discussed in the following section, there are endless reports and measurables that you can analyse to determine the effectiveness of your campaign. You will need to establish which ones are actually relevant to your marketing.

Testing & Measuring Online

As with any element of your marketing campaign, you will need to track your results and measure them against your investment. Otherwise, how will you know if your online marketing is successful?

These results - or metrics – need to be recorded and analysed so you can see how they impact your business overall and calculate your return on investment.

Some examples of metrics are:

- New account setups

- Conversion rates
- Page stickiness
- Contact us form completion

Due to the popularity in online marketing and the importance of having a strong web presence, companies have demanded more sophisticated tracking tools and metrics for their online activities. It can be very difficult to not only know what to measure, but also HOW to measure.

Thankfully, it is easier than ever to get the information you need with the many types of software and services available, including Google Analytics, which are free and can provide very good data.

Metrics to Track

The following are the key measurables to watch for when testing and measuring your internet marketing efforts:

Conversion Rates

How many leads has your online presence generated, and of those leads, how many were turned into sales? Ultimately, your campaign needs to have a positive impact on your business.

Regardless of the specific purpose of the campaign – from lead generation and service sign-up, to blog entries – you need to know how many customers are taking the desired action in response to your efforts. Your tracking tool will be able to provide you with this information

Spend

If you are not making a profit – or at least breaking even – from your internet marketing efforts, then you need to change your strategy. Redistribute your financial resources and reconsider your motives and objectives for your online campaign.

An easy way to do this analysis is to divide your total spend by conversions. This could also be broken down by product. You could also use tracking tool and view reports on the *per visit value of every click*, from every type of source. Your sources can include organic/search engine referrals, direct visit (i.e. person typed your web address into their address bar), or email/newsletter.

Attention

You need to keep a close eye on how much attention you are getting on your website. One of the best ways to analyse this would be to compare unique visitors to page views per visit to time on site. How many people are visiting, how many pages they are viewing, what pages they are viewing, and how much time they are spending on the site?

A unique visitor is any one person who visits the website in a given amount of time. For example, if Evelyn visits her online banking website daily for an entire month, over that one month period, she is considered to be one unique visitor (not 30 visitors).

You may also want to look at referring sources as well – the places online that refer customers to your website. You'll be able to determine what referring sources offer the ***best*** visitors.

Top Referrals

Know who is doing the best job of referring clients to your website – and note how they are doing this. Is it the prominence of the link? Positioning? Reputation of the referring company?

Understanding where the majority of your visitors are coming from will allow you focus on those types of sources when you increase your referral sites. They also allow you to gain a better understanding of your online market – and target audience.

Bounce Rate

The bounce rate is the number of people who visit the homepage of your website, but do not visit other pages. If you have a high bounce rate, you either have all the necessary information on your homepage, or you are not giving your customers a reason to click further. In Google Analytics, view the *content* or *pages* report and view the column stating bounce rate.

Errors

It is very important to track the errors that visitors receive while trying to access or view your website. For example, if someone links to your website, but makes a spelling error in typing the link, your users will see an error page in their browser, and will not ultimately make it to your website.

You can also receive reports on errors that customer's make when trying to type in your website address in their browser. You may wish to buy the domains with common spelling mistakes, and link those addresses to you true homepage. This will increase overall traffic and potential conversions.

Onsite Search Terms

If you have a *search website* function on your website, it is useful to monitor which terms users are most frequently searching. This can provide valuable insight into the user friendliness of your site and your website's navigation system. This information will be included in the traffic reporting tool.

Bailout Rates

If you provide users with the option to purchase something on your website (i.e. shopping cart), then you can track where along the purchasing process people decided not to go through with the sale.

This could be at the first step of receiving the order summary and total, or further when stating shipping options. By obtaining this information, a company can reorganise or revamp their website to make the sales process more fluid and possibly encourage more purchases.

Here are the three main questions you should be asking yourself when evaluating your website presence:

- Who visits my website?
- Where do visitors come from?
- Which pages are viewed?

Knowing the answers to these questions will ensure that the website fulfils its purpose of helping you to capture new customers, win more business and increase your profits.

WHAT NEXT?

'Organise and execute around priorities'

Steven R Covey (1932-2012) Author of 'The 7 Habits of Highly Effective
People'

Marketing and business is not easy. If it were, all business owners would be relaxing on a beach somewhere and we know that they're not. In reality, about eight out of ten businesses don't last five years, and, of those that do, eight out of ten probably don't last another five. But whilst having a business that provides you and your family with everything you've ever dreamed about may not be easy, it is possible. And, hopefully, reading this book has convinced you that it not only is possible, but that, perhaps with a little help, you too can make it happen.

But what are the pitfalls you need to avoid?

- Trying to do it all yourself
- Failing to have a strategy that works
- Getting bogged down with too much busy work

No-one succeeds by themselves. Just as sports professionals have coaches that work with them on the minute details of their game, business professionals can also benefit from having a coach. Your coach will guide you through the uncharted waters of your growing business, support you with appropriate expertise and advice, and keep you on track by holding you accountable for your actions.

By now you will know what it takes to have a winning strategy. Everyone has a strategy. *Wait and see what happens* is a strategy. But not everyone has a strategy that works. You need to know your target customers and understand what keeps them awake at night.

Having attracted their attention, you need to educate them about the benefits of your offering, warn them of the risks of going elsewhere and make them an offer they can't refuse. If you don't have the capability to take the prospect on such a journey, you need to innovate until you do, or else be forever at the mercy of customers looking for what they think is the best deal.

Finally, as the business owner, you must spend your time on the high-value tasks that generate the most income for your business. Usually, these are tasks that only you can do. Calling your most important clients, innovating new products or services, strategic planning for the future, meaningful discussions with your key employees. These tasks are crucial to the long term future of your business and they won't get done unless you do them. They must not be at the mercy of low-value tasks that other people could and should be doing.

You've taken the most important first step by deciding to focus on increasing your profits. Doing so will provide you with the financial headroom to invest in your business further by getting the support you need, creating a winning marketing strategy and learning how to delegate.

If you have any questions, or would like a confidential independent perspective of your business, you can contact the author at info@MaximumPerformanceAcademy.com

Also, if you haven't already done so, please visit www.MaximumPerformanceAcademy.com for more valuable business and marketing resources.